Praise for *The Zen of*

"Outstandingly good
insightful book about
SAGAR, *Climber, writer*

"Written by a climber, and for climbers, there is no better book to get you started climbing with the right mindset." —ADAM ONDRA, *first person to climb 5.15c and 5.15d, multiple World-Cup Gold Medalist.*

"Simply put, this is the best book on climbing I have ever read! In this innocuously sized, un-illustrated paperback lies an incredible density of profound, thought-provoking and deep knowledge on climbing … beautifully written by a master of the writing craft." JOHN KETTLE, *climbing coach and writer*

"A fascinating read. We are climbing our best by paying attention, on purpose, in the present moment, and nonjudgmentally to the unfolding of experience moment by moment. The book integrates different forms of practice for developing your physical, cognitive, and mental domains. Highly recommended!" —UDO NEUMANN, *climber, coach, filmmaker, co-author of* PERFORMANCE ROCK CLIMBING.

"Simple but elegant, vivid prose … An inspiring book aimed at rock climbers and other athletes that's ideal for both spirituality and sports psychology sections. Its emphasis on the virtues of cultivating mind-body awareness will also appeal to readers interested in New Age wisdom." LIBRARY JOURNAL

"If you really want to level up your climbing ... *The Zen of Climbing* is essential to creating that experience. It's a book we can all read, learn from, and then revisit time after time." —STEVE BECHTEL, *founder of Climb Strong and author of* LOGICAL PROGRESSION

"A skillful and entertaining presentation of aspects of Zen that can make one a better climber and, at the same time, enhance one's enjoyment of climbing. Top athletes ... reveal how these traits improved their performance and led to deeper understanding and appreciation of their craft." —JOHN GILL, *father of modern bouldering, author*

"A skilled and experienced climber, Francis Sanzaro writes about his long-time application of Zen Buddhist mind-training techniques to overcome the difficulties of fear and enhance performance in life-challenging, climbing situations ... The lesson: we could bring this wisdom not only into climbing and other athletic pursuits but also into modern-day life in all its many aspects." —JOHN BAKER, *co-editor of* CUTTING THROUGH SPIRITUAL MATERIALISM *and* THE MYTH OF FREEDOM

"Between the start and finish of every climb, big or small, is a vertical gulf we can see across but never fully chart beforehand. *The Zen of Climbing* provides a peerless working model of how to embrace the unknown, cross that gulf and come to know the crazy wonderful sorcery of ascent." —JOHN LONG, *author of more than forty books, storyteller, stonemaster*

IN THE MOMENT

The Zen of Climbing

Francis Sanzaro

Saraband

Published by Saraband
3 Clairmont Gardens
Glasgow, G3 7LW
www.saraband.net

Text copyright © Francis Sanzaro 2023
In the Moment series copyright © Saraband 2023

All rights reserved. No part of this publication may be
reproduced, stored in a retrieval system, or transmitted,
in any form or by any means, electronic, mechanical,
photocopying, recording, or otherwise, without first
obtaining the written permission of the copyright owner.

ISBN: 9781913393717
eISBN: 9781915089861
Audiobook: 9781913393816

Printed and bound in Great Britain by Clays Ltd,
Elcograf S.p.A.

4 5 6 7 8 9 10

*Note: Climbing grades are given in two forms throughout
this book: the US "decimal" scale followed by the European
grading system. Further information on grades can be
found on international grade comparison charts, for
example the one at mountainproject.com.*

Contents

"It is only by giving oneself up completely
to the painting medium that one finds
oneself and one's own style."
ROBERT MOTHERWELL

"Allow my body to just do what it
knows how to do."
ALEX HONNOLD

"I don't like to lose — at anything ...
Yet I've grown most not from victories,
but setbacks. If winning is God's reward,
then losing is how he teaches us."
SERENA WILLIAMS

"It is an illness to think solely of winning."
YAGYU MUNENORI

"The mental part is the hardest part and
that's what separates the good players
from the great players."
MICHAEL JORDAN

"Who was I, outside of the swimming pool?"
MICHAEL PHELPS

Preface

The Art of Attention

Your desire to climb a route, a boulder, or to accomplish any athletic goal, is often the greatest thing hindering you from doing so.

I shall explain.

A few years ago, I stood beneath a granite sport climb near my hometown of Carbondale, Colorado, an idyllic mountain town at the junction of the Roaring Fork and Crystal rivers. I craned my neck upward. I was tied in, ready to go. I took a breath. Inhale. Exhale. My eyes traced the chalk as it wove through a short dihedral system, then onto the face: a direct line of slightly overhanging crimps on red and ochre granite, slopers fashioned by a climber-god, then a boulderly crux with a so-so rest before it. A soft 5.13a/7c+, but not a gimme. An area classic for sure.

The route had been on my mind for years. I had been saving it for the onsight. It was time to stop hesitating.

The route was on the downhill side of a small corridor. The routes on the uphill side were just off vert, almost slabby, and on the downhill side they were slightly overhanging. The crag was upvalley from town about ten miles and perched on the west side of the

Crystal River, which meant in town it could be 92 degrees and have you running for shade, but here, in the late afternoon, you could be in a fleece, maybe a beanie. Lodgepole pines and Douglas fir crowded the steep hillsides. Elk herds wandered below, by the river, near the hot springs. The area has a primitive feel to it, a sense of adventure.

Jordan and I had the crag to ourselves, per the norm. Storms were threatening to kill the day, and a cold, dry wind was gusting from the west, bringing with it the scent of wildfires burning in California and New Mexico, but that made for incredible conditions. Vibes were great. I had no injuries to speak of. My knot was tied and my hands were chalked. It was time. It was possible to onsight the route, but unlikely. Still, I was going to try. I have a philosophy that you should never waste an onsight attempt. Every climb is a unique experience, and you can't relive a first impression. I was rested. I had a partner who was stoked. Everything was perfect ... except me.

"Good to go?" he asked. "Yep," I said. But that wasn't entirely true. I thought I was calm and that my nerves were gone, but sure enough the second I grabbed the first hold they peeked their head, as if there all along, hiding, waiting.

How in the f*&k did that happen? I was more than a tad concerned because, with few exceptions, nerves are a performance killer. Nerves create pressure, and no one climbs well under pressure, despite popular opinion. Rather, top climbers can turn pressure into focus. But when you are nervy, you are not climbing well. It doesn't matter who you are. As it is said, athletics is 90 percent mental...and the other half is mental.

Damn. I really wanted things to be perfect on this one.

Five or so bolts up, I fell at the crux. My mind was scattered. My nerves stiffened my body. My lack of composure expressed itself in a botched foot sequence I had known was crucial. I couldn't focus because my thoughts had been at the top of the route and enamored with feelings of doing it first try—It would be so nice. Man, that would feel good. Defeated, I got back on and made my way to the chains. I should have flashed it. I lowered.

I wasn't mad, but for the first time in my life, after climbing for nearly 30 years, it struck me that the desire to climb the route had actually been the thing preventing me from doing so. That was the beginning of a massive shift in my perspective.

I resolved to make an experiment on the spot, for my next attempt.

Don't try to do the route. Don't try to get to the top. Forget about images or feelings of success you think you will have if you do it. Your only goal is to breathe, and stay there, each move by each move. Just execute. Try hard, but not too hard. But don't panic. Relaxed aggression. Poised, but with nothing to lose. Listen to exactly what your body needs. Respond as quickly as possible. Make good decisions.

Then I remembered a trick I had heard the American phenom Chris Sharma mention years ago, a trick he used on himself to calm nerves—convince yourself you are not going to do it. Tell yourself, don't worry, you are not going to do it this time. Not this time. This is just a beta burn. This was a step further than my initial plan—don't just release yourself from the pressures of success: be sure of your own failure.

That's exactly what I did. On my next burn I clipped the chains. Despite this being a type of route I don't do second go, it felt easy. There was no flow state, nothing mystical, but I was clear, my climbing free from the pressure I had put on it. My body did what it knew how to do, without interference. Even better, it was supremely enjoyable, as if I had discovered a new way of climbing, despite having done it all my life.

Over the course of the next few months I kept doing the same thing, for sport climbing, bouldering, ice and trad climbing, all of which I partake in. I unburdened myself from expectation. As a result, my attention sharpened. I found myself enjoying climbing more, which I didn't think was possible. I got to know my body, and the language of stone, with greater intimacy and acuity. My climbing got more predictable. My endurance improved. I became more efficient. I didn't break records, but I got better, not necessarily because I got stronger, but because I had removed the most common cause for failing: lack of awareness. It was a fundamental awakening in my mental game and a shift in my mindset. As I would later learn, it was a perspective shared among top athletes, artists, and, as the title suggests, Zen masters, the latter a tradition I have been practicing all my life...just not, apparently, in climbing. The more I read and experimented on myself, the more I learned that it was, foremost, a strategy of dealing with one's mind: an emphasis on taking away and simplifying, a deployment of the power of subtractive thinking. I had simply tried it out on climbing.

I went home that day and thought about how I had sabotaged myself. And when I thought about it more, I realized that this had been a recurring pattern in my climbing career, whether it was on hard boulders, sport routes or hard ice and mixed climbs. In short, as someone who considers themselves self-aware, I hadn't been.

It came to my attention that before a send, burn or a go on a hard boulder, when I'd have to focus and get shit done, I'd get nervy. I'd be off my center, but I couldn't articulate it for the simple reason that I didn't know where my center was, nor even, if I'm honest, that I should be looking for it in the first place. It's hard to describe this state, despite it being the default state for most climbers.

For a long time, I told myself a story about nerves:

~ that it was a natural reaction. Nerves come with performance, right?

~ that they were just part of the deal. Everyone
  gets them.
~ that I needed to work against the nerves to calm
  them. They are an enemy I need to combat.
~ that they could be appeased a few minutes
  before I climbed. Moments before is the best
  time because they are most intense then.

Working with my nerves was just the beginning.
Fear, hesitation, expectation, consistency, not over-
gripping, reading sequences—it's all connected.
Nerves are just some of the weeds in the climber's
mind, whether you are a pro or newbie, but it's the
obvious place to start. I've had climbing partners who
are still struggling with taming nerves on hard sport
climbs despite having climbed twice a week for thirty
years. It is especially the case for new climbers—the
irrational fear of even taking a two-foot whipper,
stiffening up four feet off the bouldering mat, or the
fear of leading altogether. While it might seem that
nerves are neuro-muscular, and awareness is mental,
it's a false dichotomy. Nerves have a beginning and
an end, snaking through the entire spectrum of our
being. Nerves sprout in many different soils, yet we
lack the language to untangle them. Only practiced
awareness helps us figure out if our nerves come from
existential fear, performance anxiety, the ask, attachments, unfounded desires, ego.

The Paradox of Awareness

Here's a riddle. What do you have that you can't turn it off, have it in abundance, and yet it is one of the scarcest resources in the world?

The answer is attention. As Herbert Simon reminded us before the digital revolution, in 1971, an information economy consumes attention. Every company, brand and device in existence today wants your attention. Attention is our greatest resource. It is the manner, and method, in which we do things, and for that reason it is supremely unique for our daily function and elite performance. The same goes for all sports: awareness is the resource par excellence of any athlete. It is the coin through which we purchase mastery of our craft. Performance psychologists and professional coaches talk of situational intelligence, holistic field perception, kinesthetic embodiment, bodily cognition, and somatic intuition, but they are all variations of attention. Attention focused is awareness of one's shifting opponents on the field; awareness of one's limbs in space; awareness of one's fatigue. And so on. As Wayne Gretzky, arguably the best hockey player to have ever lived, put it, "my awareness was my creativity." Because it is ubiquitous, attention is the thing we think we all have, yet we seldom use it.

Climbing is the art of paying attention, of giving attention. Attention is the building block of our sport, and you will get nowhere without massive quantities of it. A beginner needs attention to get over the fear of taking a lead fall, or to calm the panic of trying hard; a top climber needs it to be creative in figuring out complex sequences, and then executing them. Climbing is equal parts jazz, improv, gymnastics, chess, weight-lifting and ballet. We need to be relaxed and aggressive, but, more importantly, we need to know how and when to deploy each, and then toggle back to our baseline. Not only do we have to give full attention to execution, but we also have to give full attention to the apparatus, namely because it is always changing (from route to route), which is not the case with gymnastics, or the long jump, or most sports. We need to see the bumps in a sloper to hold it with optimal efficiency, but we also need to "see" how a route will go in the alpine. We need to be attentive in our training, in periods of extended patience while we are projecting, or while fishing in a bad nut on a dangerous route. Most important, however, is seeing what is going on inside of us, and what is not going on.

Bill Cole, a pioneer in sports psychology, echoes the sentiment from another direction, "The ability to consistently stay in the moment when needed is what marks all great athletes and performers." I would add that the inability to be in the moment, as that which keeps athletes from achieving their potential, is an awareness error.

Paying attention is harder than you think. There is a lot of junk in most people's "moment." In fact, paying attention is the foundation of 99 percent of meditation practices, and most never progress past the beginner stage. If focusing on your breath for ten inhales and exhales without distraction is an enormous challenge, and it is, then imagine how hard it is to climb with a pure mind for minutes on end, sometimes hours, all the while completing complex bio-mechanical tasks that require memory integration, analysis, prediction and max muscular contraction. The truth is you can't, and are not going to achieve it perfectly. But you can get better, and hence get better as a climber.

Ask yourself: how is a lack of pointed attention affecting my climbing? The answer is a lot. Given that the vast majority of climbers fall on their projects or fail to improve because of awareness problems—botching a sequence, forgetting beta, missing holds, miscalibrating this or that, overtraining, undertraining, not seeing weaknesses—becoming not only more aware of your craft, but more aware in your craft, will make you a more agile, intuitive and intelligent climber. No, this isn't just about practicing mindful climbing and turning climbing into a moving meditation. Meditation is one thing. Climbing is another. It's much more complex than that. We are talking about remaking ourselves, and then, in the process, remaking our climbing. You cannot arrive at the latter without the former.

Introduction

Be Suspicious

You should be suspicious that I'm full of shit. I wouldn't blame you.

But be not worried. This book is the fruit of life-long dedications—to climbing, to Zen—which is as it should be. I've been a climber all of my life and still am: a sport climber, boulderer, ice climber, trad climber, alpine climber. When I'm not climbing, I'm running or skiing in the mountains in Colorado, or I'm writing. I was put on the cover of *Rock and Ice* magazine when I was in college, but I walked away from pursuing a sponsored climbing life to get a PhD in the Philosophy of Religion. Mainly because Zen got its hook into me when I was young, and, like all slow transformations, it took a while for me to feel the effects but the hook took hold.

Zen is the art of looking, at ourselves, each other, routes and mountains. Given all the bullshit and distraction and lying and dodging of the truth these days, Zen is cathartic in the way an enema wishes to be.

For this book, I'm going to take the back-door approach. I am going to lay out the basics of Zen, but I'm also going to focus on how climbing is *already* a Zen sport. When climbing at your limit, you need Zen. What we are doing is already Zen. In his *Zen*

Mind, Beginner's Mind, a book as classic as it is profound, D.T. Suzuki aptly noted: "Wherever there is any sign of life at all, there is Zen." If philosophy isn't a set of abstract principles but rather a *manière de vivre* (a way of life), as French thinker Pierre Hadot reminded us, simply by doing some of the work advocated here, you will be doing Zen. Philosophy is about improving our experience, and climbing is only a subset of that.

If you digest what is in these pages, you will appreciate your climbing more (or whatever sport you do), have more fun, complain less, develop better technique, and, I'm going to argue, become a better athlete.

PART I

Is Climbing a Zen Sport?

Zen isn't about being relaxed,
it's about being poised.

In 2002, a watershed paper was published in the *Journal of Applied Sport Psychology*. The paper was titled "Psychological Characteristics and Their Development in Olympic Champions." Subsequent studies have further refined the findings, but what they discovered in 2002 remains as true today as it did for ancient Stoics, Zen samurai, 9a+ climbers, and, of course, Olympic athletes.

In the paper, the trio of researchers found the following attributes to be shared among medalled Olympic athletes: "(a) the ability to cope with and control anxiety; (b) confidence; (c) mental toughness/resiliency; (d) sport intelligence; (e) the ability to focus and block out distractions; (f) competitiveness; (g) a hard-work ethic; (h) the ability to set and achieve goals; (i) coachability; (j) high levels of dispositional hope; (k) optimism; and (l) adaptive perfectionism."

The list is a roadmap for athletic excellence. But maps are often deceiving. Though the researchers never mentioned Zen and were mainly interested in listing the mental traits of Olympic champions, it begs the question—can I get some of that? I didn't discover the paper until I had a good draft of this book, but when I did read it, I had a lightbulb moment: I was writing about *all* of these things, not just listing them, but about how to cultivate them on a deep level in our bodies.

My conclusion: Zen can help all athletes improve *on every aspect of the above list*. Yes, every aspect

As regards anxiety—defined as the experience of failure in advance—it *is* possible to get to a place where your focus is so attuned to execution that single-minded attention becomes the goal rather than an outcome. When that happens, failure is redefined in your climbing as the quality of experience as opposed to the quality of goal. Distractions lose their power and constriction on performance. Zen martial artists call them "blockages."

As regards resiliency, you can develop fluidity of mind such that you *can* toggle in your climbing, a mental spontaneity allowing the mind to come "in and out" across your body, as needed, with varying intensity and precision. You recover from panic quicker, relax faster and know how to apply mind in varying degrees, whether on a WI6 smear, V8 or 5.12b/7bX big wall. Having a Zen mind doesn't mean you are relaxed and aloof—quite the opposite. It means you are poised and ready to apply whatever mind you need. It means you understand what mind is, because it doesn't mean what you think it does.

In terms of confidence ... well, you will learn that confidence is one of the most overrated mental components in top performers.

As for intelligence, you will learn to rely more on natural, or somatic, intelligence. You will learn to train your body to make intelligent decisions on its own, bypassing the cumbersome machinery of calculation thinking.

As regards competitiveness, Yagyu Munenori, a 16th-century swordsman and Zen master, says it best: "It is an illness to think solely of winning." As I learned, the main thing holding you back is the *you that wants*. The desire to win and the ability to perform your best are almost always mutually incompatible. Why is that? Strong desire creates destructive patterns of anticipation, misaligned expectation, feelings of failure and a vacillating sense of self-worth hitched to improper definitions of success.

Understanding Zen as it relates to climbing will not make you an Olympian, but it will change the way you climb. For the better. Climbing is *moving Zen*, but the simplicity of the statement—to make climbing a Zen practice—masks the complexity of the task and threatens to tokenize climbing as a romantic warrior enterprise of self-improvement (which it isn't) and leverage Zen for the goal of climbing harder. Both would be unfortunate outcomes, but both are avoidable. We can avoid them by not taking shortcuts. By going deep. By acknowledging the complexity of our inner world and the complexities all athletes experience.

All climbers need to improve in a few of these aspects:

~ climbing without fear (of falling, or failing)
~ not getting fixated

- removing sources of frustration, fear, anger, self-loathing
- fully integrating bodily movements and mind
- spreading the mind equally into the body's limbs
- concentrating mind on an appendage with rapidity
- moving without blockages
- cultivating spontaneous action with mastery
- removing ego-thought from intelligent action
- listening deeply to the language of stone and body
- removing all unnecessary baggage, such as self-importance

Each of the above is relevant to elite and beginner climbers, alpinists, boulderers, ice climbers. Each of the above is relevant to boxers, rugby players, runners, MMA fighters…in short, all athletes.

Of course, continue to do your hangboard repeaters and train with all the new gadgets and protocols. Campus, work your weaknesses, stretch. Rest the right amount. Get a coach. Diversify the types of climbing you do. The space I'm trying to carve out, however, is upstream of physical training and most "tips to improve your mental game" literature, which is notoriously shallow and composed from the mentality of inevitable failure. What I'm talking about is a full-on reevaluation of how you approach the sport, a reevaluation that will help you *fully embody*, and *discover for yourself*, what sports movement researchers describe when they talk about the importance of variability, creating biomechanical advantage, using momentum, calibrating motor control, learning when to employ contralateral movement, cultivating the performance mindset, and so on.

We are going to go to the source: mental acuity is the fastest way to train physical acuity. Being strong does not translate into better technique, or a smoother mind-body interface, but a sharp mind will flow down to more controlled movements, increased spontaneity and decreased frustration. You can buy the best shovel, but if you don't know how to dig, you won't get very far.

Zen: Big and Small Mind

Accumulating knowledge is not a
process of addition, but removal.

Zen is a type of Buddhism anchored in Japan, where it has had a profound influence, notably in art, martial arts and literature. Zen was born out of Buddhism, Indian thought and Taoism around the 6th century. Only in the 1960s did Zen begin to become prominent in the West, in large part thanks to D.T. Suzuki.

Despite great teachers, Zen is one of the most misunderstood philosophical systems in the world. For instance, it's common to say, "you gotta be Zen about it," insinuating that you need to be detached and not give a shit, a statement which is *almost* in the Zen spirit, except not at all. Zen isn't uncaring about emotions or reactions. The Zen mind is sharpened by emotions and reactions, and it needs them. Zen cares deeply about our emotions and reactions, as it is against a distracted mind that the Zen mind defines itself. Enlightenment simply means you are awake to what is going on within and without, with no delusions, no fantasies. This applies to climbing as much as it does relationships, hiking in the mountains or driving to a concert.

Zen masters are not fond of titles, ceremonies, the laborious study of scripture, or posturing for authority. Some Zen schools emphasize rituals and ways of life, but these are in each case a *means*, not an *end*. All Zen masters will tell you that formalities are empty. The rote study of scripture and memorization of sacred teachings isn't necessary. Nyoten Senzaki, a Zen monk of the Rinzai school active in the first half of the 20th century, would write:

"Remember me as a monk and nothing else. I do not belong to any sect or cathedral. None of them should send me a promoted priest's rank or anything of that sort. I like to be free from such trash and die happily."

Unlike the Western philosophical tradition that used logic to advance understanding, Zen rejects logic as a means to understand the self and the world. You cannot reason, or think, your way to *satori* (a state of awakening). In fact, logic is a liability. An attachment to logic is the result of an overactive mind, one that grasps, tries to control, one that lays an artificial, gridded map over an otherwise organic landscape.

Zen is the art of pruning the mind, and pruning oneself hurts. It's savage and ruthless. You will die a small death when you take it seriously. Things inside you deflate, ideas and self-images you hold sacred are considered liabilities rather than assets. The ground drops beneath your feet. Existential vertigo is a sure bet if you tread down the Zen path.

For climbers, you may discover you climb for all the wrong reasons and that your friends do as well. You have to recalibrate. You might discover you have never *really* climbed, despite having climbed all your life. You might discover that you have read books on the mental game of climbing but that they were just vague bullet points on "mental toughness" and exhortations to "embrace the process." You might discover you are trying to climb your way to mental health, or that you are still afraid. It's unnerving. You might discover that you try climbs way above your ability because you don't want to own up to the fact that you are not as good as you think you are. You might discover that climbing is more frustrating than pleasurable. You might discover that you are trying to create a sense of self-worth, or remove feelings of negative self-worth, in your climbing. You might discover that your head game is actually far below your physical ability, and, if that's the case, which it usually is, you will discover that it's the main thing holding you back. However, these are positive developments, because you have started to see with sobriety. All of these discoveries will be found in "small mind."

Small mind is the mind we use on a daily basis. Small mind is the mind of "I," of wants and needs, expectations, anticipation, goals, disappointments. Of big mind vs. small mind, Shunryu Suzuki writes:

"If your mind is related to something outside itself, that mind is a small mind, a limited mind. If your mind is not related to anything else, then there is no dualistic understanding in the activity of your mind. You understand activity as just waves of your mind. Big mind experiences everything within itself... Even though waves arise, the essence of your mind is pure; it is just like clear water with a few waves."

The more you deconstruct small mind, the more you inhabit big mind. Enlightenment is living from a place of big mind.

Seeing small mind at work means you have reserved attention for the things that matter, since small mind generates the majority of lapses in attention, or better, it is defined by a relation to something outside itself, as Suzuki notes, which is the essence of distraction. To climb with small mind is to be beholden to all the friction, distractions and blockages that come with it: the concepts of success, ideas, fears, pride and goals we wrap around ourselves. Once you gain some distance from small mind, something grows in its place, and that something can never be taken away. Big mind replaces small mind; big experience replaces small experience, though "big experience" isn't big, or an experience. Climbing becomes more enjoyable, less filled with stress and expectation. Words fail to describe it because words only work in the realm of small mind, but what I can say is that the way you move will change.

Sport and Immediacy

It is impossible to complete anything.

I used to think I knew, or mastered, a climb once I had done it. I'd rarely do it again. I'd move on. I had done it, after all, and I was bored with it. In truth, about the only thing I gained was confidence, and the hope, that I could do something harder. I didn't even know what I was missing. We think we know a route and can be done with it after we clipped the chains, but there is another way of navigating the world—and rock and ice—which doesn't carve up athletic experiences into fodder for our insecure egos (small minds).

Climbing isn't about completing routes. The notion of completing anything is a delusion. In reality, nothing can be completed because movement is never finished. At the most brute level, athletics is about the body in motion. Yet, there's never a time when our bodies are *not* moving. Instead, when climbing, we move *into* a type of awareness, an awareness paired with a type of movement: athletic movement. You cannot separate the two any more than you can separate rain from wet. This is literally what our game is about. It's not complicated. Climbing is a particular *type of embodied attention* applied at a certain time and place. It is only by understanding this fact that you can finally see what it is you are doing when you climb. Sending a route is simply a seal on a letter you have already written. You need to realize that to get better at climbing is to focus on writing the letter, not on the seal.

Ultimate Perfection

Without thinking, the body knows.

When the mind is clear, the moment is clear, and only then can our body do what it was designed to do. Takuan Soho, a 16th-century Zen master, wrote the following: "When the ultimate perfection is attained, the body and limbs perform by themselves what is assigned to them to do with no interference from the mind." We should add...no interference from small mind.

Soho spoke of swordsmanship, but the statement can be echoed, nearly verbatim, in the world's best climbers. In an interview with CNN, Alex Honnold—the first to free solo El Capitan, among other feats—said the goal is to "Allow my body to just do what it knows how to do. Like to not think through those steps anymore, to not think about how I'm supposed to climb, but to just climb." The opposite of what Alex is talking about—an unclear or overactive mind, which are the same thing—is making moves your body knows are inefficient, but powering through them regardless, or moving with jerky limbs, or second-guessing beta. Alex *is* thinking, of course, because ceasing your brain's activity is impossible—despite the romantic no-mind philosophy of the "zone"—it is just that he is thinking with just the right amount, no more, no less. He is practicing what we could call *skillful means*.

Not only is coordinating muscle difficult when there is cognitive interference, neuroscientists have found that muscle output decreases significantly. One paper, published in *Scientific Reports*, found that when athletes try to think and exercise at the same time, the ability to do both is compromised—we lose cognitive capacity *and* muscular performance. The loss, however, is uneven: muscles suffer the most. Muscular ability decreases 13 percent, compared to very small losses in mental function. For athletes, the action item is clear: get rid of as much cognitive interference as possible to help you perform and allow your muscles to do what they need to do. When you are trying hard routes near your limit, losing 5 percent of power will cause you to fail, much less 13 percent.

In the moment. Letting our limbs move by themselves. No interference. Right thinking. All things perfectly relevant to climbing...and muscular output. Or Zen. Or any athlete. It sounds easy enough, except it's the most difficult part of any athletic or mindfulness training.

Inner vs. Outer World

Success is a liar.

I used to think I'd be a happier person if I did harder climbs. A lot of climbers think like this. In most instances, I *was* happier. I'd set a goal and achieve it. I was proud of myself. Being proud is good. Achieving goals is good. But I was happier in the way you are after getting new gear—the magic wears off after about a week, and the gear is now dirty and in the closet. You know it's there, but you have to think about it. In short, the shelf life of a hard send in our mental store is short. Successes, and the happinesses attached to them, are disposable. We know this because soon after we are shopping for another.

Don't get me wrong, however, feeling proud after doing a hard route is good, but being proud of climbing a grade pales in comparison to being satisfied with a stellar performance. A good performance doesn't have a rating: emphasizing ratings is small mind attaching itself to something outside itself, often the site of attachment being a feeling of pride for having sent the grade. Grades are a means for the ego, or 'I,' to express itself. You can have bad and good performances, but the difference is that when you are proud of a performance, rather than a rating, you are beginning to emphasize the thing that *actually* helps you climb harder—no amount of pre-attempt desire will help you climb harder. A 5.12/7a+

climber should be just as satisfied with a good performance as a climber sending their first 5.14a/8b+. A deep sense of accomplishment is not copyrighted by those who do a sport at the elite level. In fact, thinking like this is delusional and the inertia behind so much fever-induced grade chasing in climbing—the idea that if we climb harder, we'll be happier, or become better people. If only.

The effects of this type of small-mind thinking manifests also in top athletes, who don't feel the way they had hoped after doing something hard. The 2020 movie documentary called *The Weight of Gold* is a testament in this regard. Former Olympic athlete and gold medalist David Boudia sums it up: "It doesn't matter if you are an Olympic gold medalist and you are the most decorated athlete in human history or you are someone driving a bus, you are prone to depression." *Well, yeah, of course*, you say. Still, in the back of our minds, we do think that someone who has a gold medal has a little bit of extra armor from the disappointments of the world, that is, when life sucks they can lean on that medal. But that's definitely not the case. Just like how we perceive fame, it's just a variation of 'the grass is greener.' There's no escape from deep problems with superficial solutions. There is another lesson too. More than just thinking achievements will *add* happiness, athletes think achievements can extract our unhappiness.

The more you rely on artificial achievements (grades and medals *are* artificial), the more unstable you are. The hoarding mentality is the climber's (small mind) mentality. We are stashing nuts with our successes, thinking they will help us weather the current storm or the coming one, or improve our standing in the community, or give us respect. *No, I just climb for fun,* most climbers will respond. But they are lying. Their self-worth is nearly always on the line (the perennial current storm) or the existential anxiety of needing to live life to its fullest (the perennial coming storm). In reality, the hoarder's mentality is that of avoidance and attachment, fuelled by cowardice and the inability to look closely at what we are and aren't. I.e., sobriety. A term of Buddhist philosophy, attachment is best defined by a state of being unable to detach.

Technically, from the Pali and Sanskrit *upadana*, attachment means fuel. What is it fuel for? It is the fuel of restlessness, unease, disharmony, frustration, craving for more, and so on—all forms of suffering (*dukkha*) and smallness. We can be attached to concepts, people, things, dreams, fantasies, stubbornness, sense of self, climbs, boulders, projects. When you are attached, you are not only beholden to a process or thing, your "I" becomes even more entrenched. The cycle of delusion is perpetuated, not broken.

We seek outward success and try to control things outside of us to the extent we feel out of control on the inside. As the ancient Stoics were fond of saying, all you need to worry about is what is in your control. To quote the Roman Emperor and Stoic philosopher

Marcus Aurelius: "You have power over your mind—not outside events. Realize this, and you will find strength." He doesn't mean physical strength, but mental resolve, consistency, predictable performance.

The only thing in your control is your mind: opinions, concepts, sense of self-worth, fear, doubt, and so on. A climbing performance is in your control *only* in terms of setting yourself up for mental success, not outward achievement or the final outcome, but, when you take steps toward the former, the latter will follow with more frequency and predictability.

Art of Attention

Despite being in surplus, attention is scarce.

Paying attention is a crude and, at first glance, an easy act, but one so routinely violated we can only conclude it is neither crude nor easy. Especially in our day and age when billions of dollars have materialized in gurus and digital and physical retreats with the sole purpose of getting people to pay attention, or to calm their minds, or regain control. Our era is in the middle of an epidemic of distraction. This isn't surprising, given that we live in an *attention economy*.

Long before we'd be talking about technological mindlessness, around fifty years ago little-known economist Herbert Simon wrote: "In an information-rich world, the wealth of information means a dearth of something else: a scarcity of whatever it is that information consumes. What information consumes is rather obvious: it consumes the attention of its recipients." Could this be why climbing is growing like a weed in industrialized countries? In an age of information, sports of attention—often individual in nature, where self-mastery is required for sport mastery—thrive as therapy for the illness of distraction; hence all our talk of focus as being cathartic. Which it is. Regardless, the saving grace is that cultivating attention is a "killing two birds with one stone" phenomenon: you will become better at life *and* sport.

The pop-psychology and self-help shelves of your local bookstore, should you be lucky enough to have a local bookstore, are full of 'masterclass' and 'optimization' books. Everyone, it seems, is on the improvement train. The motivations given for all this mastery are vague, if not deceitful, as if optimization itself is the reward. As if technical mastery—like climbing a big grade, or learning how to climb like Tommy Caldwell, one of the best all-arounders of all time—is a stand-in for self-mastery. But don't climb like Caldwell. Climb like you. Mastery is an act, and optimization is glorified closet organization. Mastery is not technique, but rather an understanding, a form of attention (and devotion) to a craft, a pure mind-body relation actualized in a physical skill. Lose the attention and you can only mimic a master, never become one.

The point is to level up your experience, to sync up with the real ghost in the machine: your body. Athletic mastery opens up experiences, grants freedom, and allows you to inhabit your body differently. These are the reward. The goal for any optimization project should be something that can never be taken away. Enlightenment, after all, can never be found in the bag of a thief. Big mind, like big experience, can't be stolen.

Perfection

Perfection is the art of subtraction, not addition.

'Perfection is achieved, not when there is nothing more to add, but when there is nothing left to take away.'

Antoine de Saint-Exupéry,
French writer, pilot, poet and adventurer

Antoine de Saint-Exupéry was a French pilot in the 1930s and '40s, a badass adventurer, a poet, a writer. He also wrote one of my favorite books of all time: *Wind, Sand and Stars.* Not only is it an amazing story of survival and adventure, its author was also an exceptional observer of life, aviation, and humans. His prose is deft, simple, profound.

It took me 15 years to fully understand Saint-Exupéry's concept of perfection after first reading it, and it was only when I applied it to my climbing that it rang this bell in my head. At its heart is a savage minimalism found in every corner of Zen thought, what I call subtractive thinking. In his quote, Saint-Exupéry was talking about designing airplanes, but the paradox of adding when you subtract is the essence of his observation. Big mind is what you find under small mind. As for climbing...

Perfection.
Not what you bring to the climb.
Not in the things you add.
Not in what you have when a climb or expedition is over.
It is found under everything that is taken away.
It is found when delusion has been deleted.

Hungry Ghosts

Not knowing the origin of suffering is in the desire itself.

"It is hard to even begin to gauge how much a complication of possessions, the notions of 'my and mine,' stand between us and a true, clear, liberated way of seeing the world."

Gary Snyder, writer, poet

In 2003, I traveled the world with my girlfriend at the time, now my wife. We spent a few months vagabonding in South-East Asia, then a glorious month in Burma. The Buddhism in Burma was beautiful and potent, like going to France for baguettes or Russia for Vodka. A student of philosophy and art history, I was drawn to the ancient murals, and one in particular kept grabbing my attention—an image of a wretched little creature with a tortured face, scraggly hair and a fat, rotund stomach. The creature had a curiously thin neck, his posture forever that of unhappiness—a pot-bellied, redneck version of ET. Finally, I asked a Buddhist nun what the figure was.

"A hungry ghost," she told me. Buddhist art, like Hindu art, is almost always symbolic. Those Hindu depictions of Kali or Brahman with flaming swords and 100 arms are *states of mind* and not meant to be seen as representational gods and goddesses in the sky above. The hungry ghost is a state of mind: tortured souls who cannot eat enough to satiate their appetites. They are always hungry, desirous, riveted to their stomachs, attached to the objects their base passions direct them to, but because they have such thin necks, they are never satiated. It's not about food, it's a form of living purgatory for Buddhists, because it is a state of ignorance. Ignorance about the origin of suffering is part of the staying power of suffering. We suffer because desire, by definition, can't be satiated. Unaware, we keep grasping, but there's nothing to grab. The well of desire is bottomless.

Attachments provide fleeting and unreliable benefits, like our attachments to feelings of success, which are always short-lived and never provide what we are hoping they will, i.e., deep satisfaction... because they can't. Deep feelings of satisfaction are not germinated in small mind. We are drawn to attachments on account of their fleeting nature, like putting new Band Aids on a wound every day of our lives without knowing it, and without looking for a real cure. This image of repetition is the heart of the wheel in Asian thought, because we keep circling unless we get off the ride. This is also the heart of the Buddhist notion of impermanence, the latter folded into a metaphysics of reality. Nothing is permanent, change is the only constant, and so on, which means you are not the same person you were yesterday, same with the world, same with the people you love. Acknowledging this fact unmoors you from the desire to keep things as they are, a form of control, and from putting too much stock in yourself (and your climbing) as a self-important, stable entity. As soon as we come home from a successful expedition, or the day after a send, we have a few days or a week of euphoria, but it too fades and whatever it is we were chasing in the first place comes roaring back. We become hungry ghosts. Not only are you only thinking of the next meal, you can't appreciate the one in front of you.

The hard part is that it all happens in our subconscious, with varying degrees of conscious awareness. The chatter in your subconscious robs your mind of the precious mental bandwidth to do the thing you need, or should be doing, or else processing what has happened. This might be eating that sizzling steak in front of you, or, in the case of climbing, *doing moves*. To *do moves* is moving Zen: attention in action. You are honoring the time you have given to it. You are honoring impermanence by giving attention to the fleeting quality of movement, and, as a result, you start to see small mind with greater clarity. Honoring time is an attunement to life. Doing it in climbing is a fine place to start. Your body will reward you.

Endurance

Rushing, thrashing, hurrying: attachments made visible.

'A man must not adhere to the idea of victory or defeat.'

Tesshu Yamaoka, 19th-century samurai warrior

When I first started to climb hard routes in college, at age 17, I was a strong boulderer, which meant I climbed fast, powerfully, and largely inefficiently, at least in terms of the required technique for long routes. I always felt I was up against an hourglass, and I was. The sand was falling, the pump was coming, and I climbed to avoid the pump. I wasn't relaxing into the route, as top route climbers do. I was racing through sections, diving into jugs, going from rest to rest with a panic imperceptible to my belayers, at least most of the time, but the feeling of needing to rush was part and parcel of my inner world. All this was part of a story I told myself about myself, and what I needed to do routes. I just thought it was a good strategy, which it *was* in the short term, but it was doing nothing to cultivate the mind of an endurance climber, which is not to be confused with *having endurance*. There was no peace. I was a hungry ghost, grasping for short-term success without a long-term strategy to fix the problem. I wasn't listening to the signals my body was emitting.

The strategy worked for a bit. It got me my first 5.14/8b+ but only because it was a boulderer's route. But that strategy began to fail as I tried routes that didn't cater to brute strength. I was avoiding what I needed to embrace: the slow pace, the patience a route climber needs, the search for maximal efficiency, the ability to be ok without thrusting for something: things a boulderer does not necessarily seek out. I learned that endurance isn't a simple strength located in your forearms, like a bench press is in your pecs. Rather, endurance is the result of a combination of factors, and only a deeper awareness of doing longer sequences brought that to my attention. You can hangboard and train endurance all you want, but if you are not an attentive climber, able to be in control, able to squeeze out effort with remarkable precision, able to recover from momentary panic, you won't be a good route climber.

What I had been *adding* to my climbing when I was young was a false concept of how to be a route climber. I wasn't listening to my body, to the movement. Rushing was attachment made visible. You never make good decisions when you rush either. Attachments are psychological baggage we add to our climbing out of fear we don't have enough; in short, inadequacy, lack of trust. That was me. I was building a base of endurance because I didn't even have the foresight to create one. As we say in ultra running, I wasn't "respecting the distance." We rack our gear for the lightest set-up possible—the ultra-light pack, nano biners, a puffy that weighs as much as a tennis ball—all the while allowing fear and toxic anxiety into our minds, two things that will weigh you down with 100 times more power than a quickdraw two grams heavier than another. Like trying to rid ourselves of cancer by applying no-itch creams to the rashes it is causing, we are trying to cure a disease by alleviating the symptoms. Remarkably, you can get by like this for years.

Adding is a human instinct, like squirrels stashing nuts, but it's a hoarder's mentality and, ultimately, as much of a disease as thinking a new toy, or car, will give us what we want. We don't just add shit to climbing; we also add it to life. We lug unnecessary baggage to climbing as much as to life. You might think you can arrive at the crag stressed and fragmented, distracted from bad vibes, then pull onto the rock, take a few deep breaths, suddenly be healed and get into that flow state. But that doesn't happen, and it becomes another bad story we tell ourselves. We bring jealousy to relationships if we've been cheated on. We bring anger home to our boyfriends or girlfriends when we feel disrespected. Adding and holding on is a human impulse and the overall entropy of small mind. Accumulation happens automatically, removing takes intentionality. Accumulation colors movement, and thus colors experience.

A Listicle of Attachments

Attachment is blocked vitality. It is a destructive psychological tendency in all of us.

Climbers, and I mean *all* climbers, are attached to one of the below. This is what motivates us, day in and day out.

~ to a project
~ to getting better
~ to a training methodology
~ to getting sponsored
~ to the feelings we think we will have when we arrive there
~ to being elsewhere—in the mountains, usually
~ to thinking sending our project will make our lives better
~ to thinking climbing such and such
~ a mountain will make us happier
~ to thinking the North Face of X will earn us respect
~ to clipping the chains
~ to standing on the summit
~ to avoiding failure
~ to being good.

Attachment is a psychological tendency. Parents get attached to children. We get attached to goals in life, to girlfriends and boyfriends, to ways of life, to jobs. I think at one point in my life I was attached to every item in the above list. A state of being attached isn't necessarily good or bad, in the ultimate sense, but human. It is only good or bad—we should really say effective or ineffective—*in relation* to what you are trying to achieve.

While saints and gurus might leave their families and retreat to meditation caves to rid themselves of all worldly attachments, it's not a realistic goal for us. Nor necessary. Nor even a good idea. We can take a more surgical approach—for athletes, attachments are often the biggest barriers to top performance. For example, take the example of getting better. All climbers want to get better. I do. Is wanting to get better making me worse? Am I attached? The difference is the rationale for wanting to get better. If you want to get better to climb harder routes, you are attached, and you are handicapping yourself for a variety of reasons. And that's ok. Just see it and acknowledge it. We are self-sabotaging all the time. Don't judge yourself at the moment. If you want to get better to impress other climbers, you are attached. If you want to get better at actually climbing—the act of doing moves—or at interpreting the language of stone or listening to your body—and you want this because you love to climb—then your desire isn't end-goal desire, but rather an ongoing dedication to a practice. I don't say *process* because even that can be misleading, though of course there's overlap. A process can imply a goal. A practice—which isn't the same as going to practice—is open ended. To practice means to dwell in an activity with intentionality, and it is inclusive of training, climbing, thinking about climbing, and so on. Practicing something out of a deep respect for a craft and trying to get better in said craft is the single fastest way to improve. At anything.

Attachments are blocked vitality. Attachments add texture, excitement and drama to your inner world, but, in essence, they are like looking through a dirty pane of glass to glimpse the sun better. For starters, figure out the biggest things that annoy you about your climbing, or whatever sport you do. What's the strongest emotion? What bothers you the most? Where you find it, whether it is happiness after a send or feeling like shit after a failure, you will find an attachment. Ask yourself if that emotion is helping you climb better. The answer is always, "It isn't."

The Noble Truths of Climbing

Climbing can't give you anything
unless you first give yourself to it.

Courtesy of the four noble truths, the Buddhist philosophical system states that: (i) life contains suffering; (ii) suffering is caused by desire and cravings; (iii) you can liberate yourself from suffering if you extinguish desire; (iv) you should seek the end of suffering in the eightfold path.

For climbers, attachments—often called *extrinsic motivators* in sports psychology—fold into the schema as one cause of suffering. They are results-oriented motivations, as opposed to *intrinsic motivators*, which is a form of motivation that comes from deep within us. To be extrinsically motivated is to be in the common lot, and one will argue that since it suits so many of us, what's the problem? The problem is, aside from the beneficial changes that occur inside of us when we cultivate intrinsic motivation, is that athletes across the globe, in all decades, have said the same thing: they do their best when they *focus on the game*. Athletes fueled by extrinsic motivators exhibit higher rates of burnout and depression, on account of unrealistic expectations and from spending the majority of their time attached to externalities, which are fickle and unreliable (the essence of small mind). If you must, be attached to the simplicity and humility that climbing requires. To *really* focus on the game, which means you are giving yourself over to the performance, with a focus on just performing, you can't be extrinsically motivated.

There is magic at work—the short-term happiness of thinking we are good, or the thrill of clipping chains—mask the long game of deep satisfaction in just climbing, of inhabiting movement with greater complexity. It's not what climbing gives to "you," as this is just *using* climbing, just as we use people in business or relationships, constantly trying to *extract* something from them, because all we see in them is what they can do *for us*. Like hungry ghosts, we keep adding sand, trying to fill it up—with climbing, with careerism, with materialism—until we realize the joy is in holding the sand in our hands. Or that the sand is all we really have.

Fear of Losing Talent

Your insecurities more than your strengths
will dictate how you climb.

Patrick Mouratoglou, long-time coach of Serena Williams, once wondered why athletes tank—that is, why they suddenly blow it in a big match and can't recover. Mouratoglou concluded that athletes tank because of the "fear of losing the only thing they have." What is the only thing athletes think they have? "Talent."

Most athletes are driven by the desire to succeed, success often being a public recognition, loosely defined. The public shame of not succeeding can even outweigh our personal sense of failure. How many of us have been in a gym or on a crag and not tried hard out of the fear that we won't succeed—i.e., our real ability will be exposed? I'm guessing everyone needs to raise a hand.

In college, I climbed with this guy who would never try something he was capable of doing. We'd warm up, and then he would thrash around on something three or four grades above his limit. He would fail on V9/7c+ boulders regularly instead of enjoying V5/6c's comfortably. I'd never say anything. Whatever floats his boat. In the six years I climbed with him, he never sent over V5/6c. Most of the time, however, he threw himself on problems he had no chance of doing. At the time, it perplexed me.

Why was he trying something too hard for him?
Didn't he get tired of failing?
Didn't he see, like the rest of us, that he'd never do it?
Didn't he want to get that feeling of success once in a while?
Didn't he know that to improve, you have to build confidence, and to build confidence, you need to have a solid base of sends?

I never got answers to any of these questions until later, when I realized that what he was bringing to climbing dictated how he climbed (a story he was telling himself *about* himself: an attachment). He was afraid of losing the inflated sense of talent he thought he had. His self-worth was at stake. This dynamic can get the best of all of us, without exception. If we are insecure and trying to prove something to ourselves or others, we tend to climb with impatient aggressiveness. If you are overconfident, you climb with a muted over-zealousness. If you are overly controlling, you freeze when you exit your comfort zone. If you have no care in the world about succeeding at your full potential, then you might just go top-roping in the gym and call it good. Perhaps you don't believe in yourself, or you never try things at or near your limit because of a lack of vision, a situation just as harmful as having too much.

At Rifle, one of my home crags, climbers up and down the canyon, at all levels, are all-too-frequently on climbs where they don't belong. It's obvious to everyone but them. Like Mouratoglou said, they are fearful of feeling like a failure, of losing a sense of success. There's a difference, of course, between pushing your boundaries and delusion, and we are the only people who know the line with any exactitude, but, what is beyond doubt is that when you can climb your worst in public, be ok with it and develop an honesty with yourself, is coincidentally when you can climb your best, because it takes the same amount of mental transparency (sobriety about one's ability) to let yourself climb your hardest as it does to let yourself fail in public. This is because to climb your hardest you need to *just climb*, and to climb your worst is also just *to climb*. FOPO, or fear of other people's opinions, is a phrase coined by sports psychologist Michael Gervais. As someone who works with top athletes on a daily basis, he'd be the first to tell you that not only is it common among top performers, it is just as common among all athletes, and it's debilitating. Writes Gervais: "If you really want to conquer FOPO, you'll need to cultivate more self-awareness." The key is being ok with the flux of performance, of good days and bad days, good conditions and bad conditions, and with routes that fit you vs. routes that don't. When you try to force a performance, you create a pattern of hijacking your body. It is like striking a dog. You lose its trust eventually.

Talent is a concept athletes attribute to themselves, a concept because, like all concepts, it is a prism through which something is understood. Mainly, we understand our "I," our core identity, through this prism. At base, we all want to believe we are talented, and who doesn't really want to think that? On the other hand, thinking you are talented has allowed many athletes, myself included, to work just a bit harder, to trust that all the training will result in something. Thinking you are talented and have what it takes keeps you going, gives hope. Right? Kinda.

But of course, as Mouratoglou has seen in working with the world's best, an athlete will self-sabotage (a variation of choking) rather than lose—because when you self-sabotage, you are in control. Having a robust "I" necessitates control. When you lose control, the "I" is unmoored, and that's unsettling. When you choke, you are losing for a reason you are aware of, *in control of*, the assumption that being beaten fair and square could dislodge your inflated sense of self, which, if you are a choker, is based on an unhealthy attachment to outward success. The "I" only exists in relation to the outside. Rather, you need to focus on what's in your control, and yet refrain from being controlling. When you choke, you are both giving up and holding on too tightly. You are not allowing yourself to see the reality of an actual loss, but rather reacting too quickly to the incipient idea of losing, as it is only in an honest assessment of the opponent and potential defeat road climb—where solutions and countermeasures present themselves. When we choke, fear of loss of self grips us, robbing our minds of analytical and creative bandwidth through which we might change the course of events.

While we all have a sense of stable identity in the form of a self, it frequently becomes inflated. When inflated, we call it an ego. Climbers try only as hard as their egos allow, and our egos dictate how we approach training and all things climbing. You'd think if you have an insecure ego, you are always just trying hard all the time, but sometimes the opposite can be the case—you don't try hard enough because you don't want to know your limit. And when you find your actual limit, it's depressing because you thought you were a V12/8a+ climber. You try hard to pretend to be by getting on easier climbs or trying a lot of V12/8a+ climbs but never really trying, and so you rationalize away your failure on them by saying you never gave them your *all*.

Denial, as attachment made visible, is a powerful motivator for *not seeking*. Often, the fear of succeeding comes from the avoidance of acknowledging that we are not as good as we think we are. Remember cosmic insignificance therapy: your climbing does not matter. It has no ultimate significance for the world. We need to take a sober look at ourselves and embrace what we find. What we find is not good or bad, but the right footing, and unless you find the right footing, real improvement will always be a matter of grasping and half-heartedly implementing the latest training program, the shortcuts to strong fingers, and so on.

Drive

Drive indicates success, but sometimes you need to change the driver.

Research has proven that one of the best indicators of success in athletes is *drive*. When you think about what we mean by a *driven athlete,* it's odd the image is one of a car: a butler and driver. An athlete is in the back seat being driven by *something*. Some are driven by a person named Win, others by a chap named Gold Medal. Some are driven out of a fear of failure. Win, Gold Medal, Failure—to be driven by these, or another, is to inhabit a *state of mind* and take on the characteristics and behaviors of what you think it takes to achieve them. From the goal, we back up into a position and organize the chips accordingly, such as our training, food, mental prep. The rub—it's not going to be an ideal state of mind.

You need to figure out what drives *you*…and don't just accept the situation if the driver isn't who you want it to be. You *can* change the driver. Most need to. You need to interrogate them. Most athletes are driven by the same thing the entirety of their lives, which means the "deepest" source of their energy remains unquestioned. As with all things, when something is unquestioned, it is controlling you. In other words, the most indicative motivator for top performance is out of your control. Read that again.

In an interview, sports psychologist Jim Loehr noted that while many athletes are driven by an impulse to be better than the competition, when he sat them down and asked what they'd *really* like to motivate them, it was the love of the game. The athletes admitted that the desire to win often got the best of them, but it never felt good. They knew it's more satisfying, and sustaining, to be driven by dedication to the craft. One thing we forget is that this is why sports exist—because athletes love doing the activity itself. Remove that and the train stops, the sport goes extinct. And throughout history many sports have gone extinct. Personally, I am in love with climbing. Since I was 12, I have been enamored with all aspects of moving over stone and ice. I still want to climb hard, to continue to master the craft—and I have a long way to go—but the act itself has only one real moment: the moment you are doing it. The rest is distraction, at best, and, at worst, dishonest. If the simplicity of the act doesn't sustain you, day in and day out, change the driver. Climbing goals are not the ultimate enemy. Set yourself goals, but hold them lightly. Let them work for you, rather than you them. Let the 'small' goal, if it is a grade or objective, motivate and inform the 'large' goal: a deeper engagement with self and body through sport.

Thinking you will become a happier person by climbing harder is only effective if climbing caused your unhappiness in the first place, which it rarely does. Climbing *can* cause unhappiness, for example if you continue to fail on a project for too long or you leave home for months on an unsuccessful expedition. You *can* calm your frustration over a move by *doing* that move, for instance, but doing a move won't make you feel better because you cheated on your boyfriend. You can't squeeze apple juice from an orange: you can solve a problem at the level it was created, but you can't solve a complex and constant source of frustration. To solve that, you need to go above the level. You need big mind.

Sports are crude mechanisms, and no act, thought or way of moving is more privileged than the other. Surfing a big wave, paddling down a river, or skiing a remote peak is no more inherently psychoanalytic than playing croquet or drinking tea. It is all *practice*, and simply getting to the point where you can let it be practice, and not something else, is a profound shift.

The Summit

It is at the top where you find the bottom.

I remember watching a TV show about a billionaire who developed his own private island near New York, adjacent to Manhattan. It took him years of painstaking work to build. He spared no expense. Then he finished it. Standing there, on film, pondering the sea and his new home, said he had expected to have great thoughts on his private island. But, after the last construction worker left the site, it turned out nothing had changed. He still had the same old thoughts. After a few months, he sold the place. He looked sad. He had expected so much.

We're lucky as climbers. The places we go are inspiring, the stuff of billboards and multi-million-dollar commercials—desert towers, ribbons of ice, soaring ridges and cliffs of blue limestone. The climber's terrain is idealized, given the romanticization of the summit. As far as nature is concerned, the Western imagination is 'topophilic' (in love with place). The earliest goals in climbing—in the 1800s and first half of the 1900s—were predominantly those of being the first to stand on top of something. Such was the case for Mont Blanc, the Matterhorn, then into Alaska, the Himalayas. Climbers were "conquerors," and the visual iconography in that time was one of a general marching into battle along with his soldiers (and porters). Then, after most peaks were topped out, alpine climbing moved to more technical faces while, starting in the 1970s, rock climbers and boulderers found *difficulty* as a reward. In America in the 1950s and '60s, however, John Gill's focus on form and inner feeling was an exception. Gill, with a modest background in gymnastics, viewed climbing, and especially bouldering, more in terms of gymnastics than anything else. For Gill, grace in execution was paramount.

The top is a legacy of climber-thought, drawn from our deep history, popular imagination and our own romantic leanings that overcoming difficulty, and hence, achieving a new level, is the main goal. The problem is that climbing is equally expressive—a dancer would not go to the studio and consider it a good day if they only did a hard sequence, as if, once they had done it, they could move on to another hard sequence. A dancer wants to feel flow. A dancer wants to be in it. The dancer wants to become the dance, to merge with their body. A dancer chases a feeling, a state of bodily affairs. Ueli Steck, the late Swiss alpinist and holder of multiple speed records up the most dangerous alpine faces in the world, including the North Face of the Eiger, once said: "Mountaineering is a transient experience. I need to continuously repeat it to live it." Steck is right. Doing a difficult alpine climb is satisfying, but it's a label post-performance, and, hence, a dull concept we apply to something beautiful and timeless. We too build our private islands—visions of success—and we convince ourselves that once we achieve it, we'll be like the billionaire. We'll stand on the shores of our hard sends and be different people, have better thoughts. But that's never the case. We are chasing ghosts. It is better to go into a hard project, or trip, convincing yourself that doing such and such a route will *not* change a thing about you, or your life. Do that with climbing, and your trip changes. For the better. Do it with the rest of life, and you are starting to taste Zen.

What's In a Name?

Naming calls something into existence,
but it also introduces the desire to possess.

The "top" and "names" are a curious pair in climbing's history. It is a strange thing to give a climb a name. Trails have names. Big mountains have names. Sub peaks usually don't have names, same with hills. Chossy cliffs don't get names, while cliffs with good rock and routes are called crags. Rivers have names, but streams and creeks don't always. We give names to ourselves and animals. Gymnastic tricks, like skateboard tricks, have names. Some houses have names, others don't.

Naming, and language, is the domain of small mind. Giving a name calls something into existence, brings it out of the morass of objects and experience. Naming is a process of appropriation by humans, an entrance into the domain of language, and through language, into meaning-making. Like the fashioning of a tool from a tree, naming is a creative act. Yet when something has a name, it tends to create the desire to possess it, in part on account of it being invested with meaning and parameter. Climbing is a sport obsessed with names. Names are how we identify, signify and communicate our shared cultural history, and, as recent naming controversies make clear, names are mechanisms of exclusion. Names tame the wild. Names mask. Names are the coin of climbing's social and cultural capital. We think we know a patch of land if we have visited the national park that encompasses it, and we say, "Yeah, I've been to such and such a park." Names (of routes, boulders or mountains) are the most obvious form of consumable attachment.

The point here, however, is not that routes are contrivances and names even more so. That much is obvious. Rather, a route is nature commodified, packaged for our climbing consciousness, whereas a route isn't such a thing to an animal, or a tree. Animals use landscapes to react to, practically. Landscapes are mediums. Landscapes turn into abstract ideas (for achievement, for social signification) only *for us*. The key is to become aware of what happens *to us* when we ingest the climbing product—when we name the experience with our labor we cloak it with abstraction, thereby suppressing a more primal connection of body to landscape, because that is what's at stake here. With an unhealthy attachment to names, we reinforce the very thing keeping us from knowing landscape with more intimacy, the latter also the medium for our improvement as climbers. Pro climbers do it instinctively—they connect to landscapes (of which crags and rocks are a subset) on an intimate level. This is, in part, why they are the best. They know how to listen with their bodies. Don't aim to get familiar with a route. Become intimate with how to move over a certain type of stone, in a certain place, and then the rest takes care of itself.

Climbing is an interaction between a body and geology. French philosopher Gilles Deleuze wrote on *becoming* rather than *being*. Deleuze sought to capture the moments of life in transition and wasn't content to define the attributes of being in 'traditional' philosophy. For climbers in the act, we are party to a becoming-geological of the body and a becoming-carnal of geology. These subtle shifts happen in micro-moments and are in constant flux. To feel these moments is magic. Cliffs become modified for our bodily transport (sharp pockets filed, bolts and chains for safety, chalk to add friction, etc.), and our minds become trodden by the traits of stone (after we leave, we rerun the climbing in our minds; our skin thickens on abrasive rock, and so on). We are purchasing experiences with our effort, trading this for that when, in reality, we should be *experiencing* something that removes the barriers to practice, not adds to them.

Cruel Exchange

Feelings of success come at the expense of others' failures.

If you make climbing about ego and one-upmanship, you *will* get an ego boost, and you *will* feel superior to another climber because you have climbed such and such a thing and they haven't. This is a feeling we have all experienced, and a rather seductive one at that, but ultimately unsatisfying because your benefit is merely reactionary and fleeting. As Suzuki reminds us, "If your mind is related to something outside itself, that mind is a small mind, a limited mind." If the point is to develop a consistent base of performance, where the joys we receive are not reliant on factors outside of our control, then we need to rely on something more than a quick hit. An ego boost is *reactionary* and *relative*.

Reactionary because we are only reacting to the failure of another. The feeling is based on what you didn't do (their failure), rather than what you did (your performance). While for some it might just be *all the more* satisfying because of another's failure, the satisfaction is fleeting because there's always someone to beat, which means the target keeps getting kicked down the road. Eventually, success on this model is shallow and unpredictable because relying on another's failure is unsustainable. That is not in your control. If your feelings of worth are tied to something you don't control, then the metric in which you define what it is you do is being led by someone who knows nothing about you. This is quick reward and quick reaction, short-term (small mind) mentality, and, if it were financial bonds, you'd be shorting yourself and tying your stocks' worth to another.

Relative because the excellence of your climbing is only in relation and not absolute. This isn't to say some athletes perform better when trying to outdo an opponent or from fear of losing—all solid motivations for any die-hard competitor—but if you are only competing against others, you are not expanding your real potential because you have created an artificial goalpost. The *real* goalpost might be elsewhere. Your body knows it. You know it...when you have one leg tied up, because that's what it is, a self-imposed handicap. Most people compete with others out of fear—they are afraid of competing against the only thing that really matters: themselves. Moreover, the language of competing against oneself is ill-conceived. You can't compete against yourself. That's impossible. What we mean when we say the phrase is that inside our minds there are competing impulses and a fragmented state of mind, such that, for example, one aspect wants to give up when another doesn't, or, in the case of doubt, one aspect thinks you can't do it, while another thinks you can. The whole conversation happens in small mind, and you can only compete against yourself in small mind.

Copyright on Enjoyment

The art of a mindful body is the art of elite athletics.

Elite climbers are no more satisfied with their sport, nor do they enjoy it more, than average climbers. A pro surfer has no more fun than an average one. But there *is* a caveat: a seasoned athlete embodies the *possibility* of deeper affects as a result of their trained body, which can lead to a richer, more meaningful experience.

When you have muscle and neural memory in certain movement patterns, the body provides a potpourri of sensation a beginner does not have access to—namely, climbing gracefully creates pleasant sensations in the body that climbing clumsily does not. Give a beginner a javelin, tell them to toss it, and their focus will be on gripping the thing and trying to throw it as far as possible. Throwing the thing won't feel very beautiful. Their minds are riveted to base execution. Their bandwidth of attention is taken up by the mechanical complexities of completing the task. As for climbers, a beginner applies too much strength at the wrong time, ignores their footing, overgrips, undergrips: a sense of awareness in and of the movement is inaccessible. They are overthinking it. Underthinking it. A first-time javelin thrower might like it, but they don't experience *deep joy* in tossing it. Give the javelin to an expert, and they will *also* concentrate on execution, but their bodies know the basics, which loosens attentional space for a deeper engagement with the movement, like being able to watch a beautiful film without having to take notes. Because it is an experience, and all experience has shallow and deep forms of engagement. All athletic movement has levels of engagement as well. It is this deeper engagement that builds craft, practice and mastery. Top athletes in any sport are able to apply no more, nor less attention than is needed. This is the age-old formula for your own quest to be a better athlete.

To borrow a term from critical theory, a seasoned athlete is more *affective*, affect defined as potentiality to feel, a state of being receptive to the energies the body and world provide. Affect is a pre-verbal possibility in which we can be moved. Affects are not feelings or emotions but indicators of our ability to be moved by the former. Top athletes have the potential to be deeply affected by movement because of their psychosomatic investment in a specific set of movement patterns. Movement is memory, and memory spans the spectrum of cognitive functions because it is the inter-connective tissue of temporality: memory spans time like nothing else can. Movement for seasoned athletes is an echo chamber where previous movements come alive, where they interact with the present, where they built the future. Where they analyze, compare, get drawn into the well of the body's deep psychosomatic history. It's just a fact of movement that athletes move with deep history in their muscles, thought patterns and tendons. Muscles produce feelings. Doing something well is not just a concept we give to ourselves, such as "It sure feels good to be good," and that's the reward. Rather, it is autotelic, which means the purpose of doing something well is sufficient unto itself. The reward is in the moment, and, for that reason, a concept cannot capture it.

The Project

A project isn't a route. A project is something
climbers do to animate non-living things.

Few sports have such a thing as *the project,* or
whatever the equivalent might be. Other athletes
have tricks they want to do, feats they are working
toward, or routines they are trying to get dialed, but
the project is unique to sport climbing, dry tool-
ing, and bouldering in particular. The project is a
gymnastic routine that, if we were gymnasts, we'd
travel around the country visiting gyms to do routines native to that *one gym.* I have projects at every
crag I visit, and they are often why I keep coming
back. Most climbers I know are obsessed with their
projects. They will warm up and get on their project
immediately...and repeat this process for entire seasons. I'm guilty, still am, but my relation to a project
is now different.

The project is something we think we can do, something we *believe* we can do, and, as such, we throw
ourselves into project mode, hoping our gamble
pays off, the 'market' being time, weather and, most
essentially, ourselves. To be in project mode means to
be focused, to put all of one's energies into one goal.
A project is an investment in the future. Yet there's
a problem here. Most climbers are bad investors—
they *want* too much, *desire* too much, and so miscal-
ibrate their ability, or, conversely, they deny they are

'projecting' because they are terrified of admitting to the complexity of the relationship. Or perhaps they are not as good as their self-image. Wishful thinking is also at play when we project, and the former is not limited to climbing. What Elon Musk, founder of SpaceX and Tesla, has to say about wishful thinking applies to projecting: "One of the biggest mistakes people generally make, and I'm guilty of it too, is wishful thinking. You know, like you want something to be true, even if it isn't true. You ignore the real truth, because of what you want to be true. This is a very difficult trap to avoid." It is a difficult trap to avoid because of the mechanics of desire.

Because it is an investment, the project is also a *projection*, necessarily involving a temporal delay of one's (ego) worth, which, as many of us know, is the biggest problem with the project, as Musk notes— the main investment isn't really time, but into a sense of self, an identity, a way we define ourselves. This isn't always bad, but it often is. We say a person has ego when they value their own self over others, or they have an inflated sense of self, and so on. The problem with the project is that it all too often builds ego into our 'self,' the motivation being an expected ego boost, or a secure identity. Rather than project out of the love of the craft, we lean onto a project for something we *don't have*, which never arrives. Break the cycle by asking yourself two simple questions: does it matter if you fail? If it does, why?

Repetition with a Difference

Where sameness is masked as difference,
you are catfishing yourself.

The 'novelty' we experience from clipping the chains or standing on top of a peak is, in fact, the polar opposite: *the same*. Theorists and philosophers who write about postmodern capitalism talk about sameness and difference, specifically sameness *masked* as difference. The products we purchase are the *same*, with only minor differences: fifteen types of peanut butter in your supermarket is a case in point. Capitalism is fueled by individualistic desire—the reason we keep buying—and yet our desires are never fulfilled because desire cannot, on principle, be fulfilled, which is why satisfaction is always delayed. But we go on purchasing because we believe satisfaction is close. The cycle is basic animal behavior.

Because the only permanent aspect of our existence is impermanence, we are always in flux. We are, essentially, a project. Coincidentally, Buddhism takes direct aim at desire in its second noble truth: suffering is caused by desire. For climbers, *sameness* is an experience we buy through effort—because experiences can be products as well—but unless that experience is applied deep in our psyches, we need to repeat it, but with a slight difference: a new climb, new project, new road trip, which is infused with a new promise. In short, you are catfishing yourself.

In fact, we suffer the lack of integration that sameness generates. The value of athletic experience is in what can't be captured by our small snares, by what can't be traded in small-mind mentality. It is all the more valuable because the deeper experience is elusive and because we can't bring it down to our size. It is big experience, as opposed to small. Because that's what happens when you try to possess—the original intensity is caged, suppressed, made small, catered for egoistic desires. You get out of it only a fraction of the potential. You decrease your affective ability. You handicap your ability to be open to new ways of moving over stone. You blunt your ears to the language of movement. It is only when you unpackage experience, by removing intermediaries (attachments being a type) and outcome-oriented thought, when you approach big experience, or, we should say, this is when big experience comes into view. Big mind is not added to anything, just as flow in movement is always there. We just find creative ways to block it, to disable it.

Erasing Art

*The art of erasure ensures that creative
perception is highest priority.*

American poet and artist Jim Dine put on retreats and clinics. At the end of each day, he told his students to erase what they have done. The students are always shocked, if not offended. They look at him weirdly. They hesitate.

Did he say what I think he said?

They are puzzled.

WTF?

They look at each other.

This is my best work.

This is what I paid for.

Yes, he did say that.

Erase it all.

With great reluctance, the students erase eight to twelve hours of hard work in seconds. After a few days of working and erasing, however, Dine has made his point—most artists are too attached to the outcome and not enough on drawing. His first point: when you are figure drawing, what matters is looking, looking carefully and patiently, and not caring what the result looks like because if you look carefully enough, the result takes care of itself. And another thing happens: the act of looking becomes the priority, and hence, you become a better artist because you are a better "looker." Riveted attention to the task is the goal. His second point, implied in the first, is that it is natural to be future-oriented and let attachment take hold. We often default to that position. After you have internalized the art of looking, only then, at least in terms of realistic drawing, can you take liberties in attention, that is, you can (like an expert javelin thrower) explore style in the execution. This happens because you have the bandwidth.

The history of Zen art testifies to the power of internal awareness, because listening is subtracting. Clearing the mind from any preconceived notion of what you think you need to paint allows that per fect moment when the brush brushes itself. D.T. Suzuki wrote of Zen art, "Technical knowledge is not enough. One must transcend techniques so that the art becomes an artless art, growing out of the unconscious." Calligraphy, of which Zen art has a long history, seeks that moment when the artist's arms and hands move without cognitive distraction, and it is said it can take a lifetime just to perform the simple task.

As a climber, when you start 'erasing' like one of Dine's students, you need to develop deep patience. It can take years, but the payoff is tremendous. In place of thinking that you will either succeed or not, always a very imprecise way of thinking, awareness needs to be on the only thing that matters—execution. Strategy is execution as well, but to pull that off, you need your base layer of execution to be seamless. In his process of doing the world's second V17/9a at Red Rocks, the Colorado-based climber Daniel Woods described to me in an interview how he had to learn the art of erasure, of removing attachment from the outcome: "At first I was too consumed about the send, rather than just flowing with the move, like taking it move by move and focusing on my breath...and I'd be like, man, this could be the one or this could be the one, you know, I was too. I was too focused on the send rather than being present. And I had, like, we had probably a week and a half where I just had that feeling. And then suddenly, I just had to flip my head and be like, *look like, every, every day now is just a session, we're going to start and just see how far we can get*. I think I just told myself every time to just see how far you can go, like, create, like, focus on your flow, focus on your breath. Like, create a good rhythm and have fun on it. You know, like, you're climbing on a line that has sick moves. It's hard. It's challenging, but just have fun, you know. And when I started getting into that mentality, all that pressure kind of vanished, and I just, I was climbing better on it." Wood's experience grew because he took away.

Sunk Cost Fallacy

The frustration pressure points indicate places where we need to let go.

Last season, I climbed a lot with a friend at Rifle, and he kept using bad beta. I was like, "Hey man, try that pocket instead of the crimp." It was a hard route, and the crimp he was using was total shit, and about a V8/7b sequence, while with the pocket it was cruiser V5/6c. I'd say it casually so as not to seem like I was the know-it-all, because we all know that guy at the crag. My friend knew it was better beta, but he would shrug and give an expression of resignation, to express he was committed to his sequence and that at this point, it was out of his hands. "I know," he'd say. Then, after weeks of getting shut down, he tried the new beta out of desperation, lowered to the ground and sent the route on his next go, the new sequence giving him enough reserve to power through the lower crux and to the chains.

Behavioral economists like to cite the *sunk cost fallacy* to explain why people continue to invest in something, or continue a behavior, even though it is a bad bet and they are made unhappy by the decision. Bad beta is a phenomenon of the sunk cost fallacy.

It is a funny thing to press on for days, perhaps weeks, with bad beta, *knowing* it is bad beta, *watching* your friend do it with better beta, *certain* their beta is best for you, but, for some reason, never actually trying the new beta. Attachment to moves is attachment to one's effort. The freedom of mind to fully release from any sequence takes more mental effort than it does to suppress, a fact of psychology because suppression and denial are easier than facing the problem in question. Simple stubbornness? Yes, but the latter indicates being stuck, and being stuck is a manifestation of attachment. Long-time climber and training coach Eric Horst is clear on this point: "The first key strategy is flexibility of perspective." In climbing, flexibility of perspective is just that—not getting stuck, remaining open. In life, flexibility of perspective is much harder, but you can't truly have it in climbing if you don't first have it in life.

The sunk cost fallacy is also the Achilles heel of alpinists and mountaineers, who, for example, might find themselves staring down four difficult mixed pitches to the summit with a storm coming in, and so decide, against all good judgement, to press on without a bag, stove and bivi gear. A clear mind starts rappelling. An unclear mind is dominated by all the things attached to the decision...*we are this far...we are so close...we have taken flights, buses, time off work. I don't want to go home empty-handed.* This is what is sunk in the sunk cost fallacy: the concepts are driving our action. We have things "sunk," that is, "baked into" the climb that shouldn't be there. Of course, folded into any decision is the mythology, the allure of the summit. Sometimes you have to go for it, however, but luck is not a strategy and your decision needs to be guided by deep intuition. A clear head allows you to grow old as a climber, more so than anything.

Shokunin

*The craft of climbing is grounded
in understanding, listening, and freedom.*

In Sukiyabashi Jiro's sushi restaurant, an apprentice will spend ten years just cooking rice. Ten years.

Why? Because that's how long it takes to master the art of rice.

Jiro Dreams of Sushi is a phenomenal movie that tells the story of Jiro. It is a masterclass in awareness, patience, mastery, and, of course, sushi. But it's only about fish insomuch as James Cameron's *Titanic* is about a shipwreck. Jiro's restaurant is unironically situated in a Japanese subway station, and the Zen themes of patience, mindfulness, awareness and constant improvement are in full view.

There is a word in Japanese for this 'genre' of person, a *shokunin*: a person who does the same thing every day. A person who surrenders to mastering the simplicity-in-complexity. The craft. One who is devoted, all-in. Jiro is considered to be one of the best sushi chefs in the world. Complexities aside, the best climbers are a type of *shokunin* without knowing it. The Yosemite Stonemasters were *shokunin*: they spent their lives mastering the craft of climbing, the art of movement. Adam Ondra, the Czech climber responsible for sending the world's first 5.15c/9b+ and 5.15d/9c—also considered the world's best climber, for good reason—is a *shokunin*. What is cultivated in the *shokunin* is a depth of understanding. In that depth of understanding is freedom.

The term yoga is a derivative from the Sanskrit root *yuj*, meaning "to yoke." In that freedom is the ability to move without hindrance, and, without contradiction, to be yoked to your body. Or better, to be unified in body and mind. Freedom and being bound to a body, the latter helplessly in the moment, are the same. The body is a teacher, of and in time. In this freedom, there are the constraints of mastery, an obsession when seen from the outside, but, from the inside, a constant looking, paying attention, listening, tweaking—being present, taking risks. What motivates a *shokunin*? A deep love and affection. Loyalty. Patience. Respect for the material. Dedication. Doing the act is enough. Autotelic. The same with us, if not for the reason it's essential to climb hard. As the German coach, filmmaker and climber Udo Neumann writes, "The hardest problems not only demand to somehow manage all the moves but also demand that we also love them." There is great truth in this statement.

Listening to the rice at each moment...for ten years. It seems preposterous, almost as ridiculous as Paul Cézanne, the French painter, taking 100 sessions, or around 500 hours, to paint an apple. *An apple*. It's preposterous until you consider they aren't trying to go anywhere.

Intermission

Weeds of the mind never stop growing. In fact, they grow faster when ignored.

Zen is nothing if not a body of wisdom instructing us to become our own mental gardener. Zen lays out the path to liberation, compassion and selflessness. Climbing does none of these things, but, then again, neither does cooking rice, and Zen is adamant that cooking rice, or chopping wood, is just as valid as anything in trying to understand the basic nature of our mind. Why? The process is irrelevant. The quality of attention, the quality of self-awareness. These are what matter. The whole is present in each part, as they say.

Of course, climbing can just be a workout, a time to chat and sip coffee and burn down the clock on the day, but that is like going to the Himalayas and playing video games at K2's basecamp. Why not use the sport as an activity that can actually benefit you and your climbing? We are not trying to become romantic warrior-climbers on a precious journey to climbing and self-realization. We are trying to get smarter and climb harder.

Zen instructs you to pay close attention to what is going on: around you, inside your mind, inside your body. Socrates, one of the greats in Western philosophy, was fond of saying that philosophy was about knowing thyself. Introspection. Digging in. Zen concurs, though with a 'small' caveat—the self at the bottom doesn't exist (small mind) and is a convenient mirage that has snowballed courtesy of the entropy of life, and only when you see the mirage can you break through.

PART II

Routes. Moves.

A route takes on a gravity in our minds,
but movement is weightless.

For a long time, I thought a route or boulder problem was the thing I was looking at. Or trying. Or falling on. It had a beginning and an end. Between that beginning and end was try-hard. The idea was to put in a good effort and send it. That's the goal. Get the goal and feel good, then set a new goal. Get better. Feel better that I'm getting better. Do this until I get too old to climb hard, then figure out a new plan. Most climbers think like this, yet it's a flawed way of thinking. It is small-mind thinking, and therefore a small experience. We are making ourselves, and our effort, instrumental. We are pimping ourselves out for something other than climbing. The essence of small mind is when it is related to something outside itself. Mind, in its essential nature, contains everything, and is therefore deformed when fixated. We see our own deformation in the way we approach routes.

A route or problem is an athletic performance—that performance is the sum of moves over a duration of time. Those moves are often broken up into sections. You try to climb to the "rest," and then there's a punchy section, then a final crux. In alpine or trad climbing, it's broken up into pitches or big features. Climbers discriminate and partition these moves, but in reality, a wall is unbroken, just as in nature there's no such thing as the border between Russia and Poland. It's a construct, not a physical border. A concept. That's obvious, but what is important is that insofar as borders are artificial, so too is movement. We never stop moving. Climbing is just a different form of movement. Movement never stops. Athletics is a ritualized movement, in a ritualized place, which we all agree to enter based on certain stipulations, boundaries and cultural agreements. Meanwhile, despite our attempts to control it, life thrusts itself in, through, and around us at all times. Change accompanies us at every turn. Taoism, of which Buddhism has become philosophical friends for centuries, speaks of chi energy as being in a natural state of ceaseless flow, and only when it stops does it lose its properties. A Taoist monk's goal is to chase the flow as it moves, not arrest it. Zen has little tolerance for talk of mystical energy, but the base understanding as it relates to climbing is the same: it is only when we think holistically can climbing movement, or any act, get the proper respect it deserves. Why respect, you might ask? That we have to ask that question is indicative of our ignorance.

It's natural that the complexity of climbing movement occludes a simple approach. Each move we do is an articulation of our limbs in coordination with our will, neural patterns, muscle memory, and complexified by our emotions. The analytic pit may seem bottomless, and overthinking is to be expected, but returning to the beginning, what often holds climbers back is the sheer *presence* of a route. The weight of it on their psyches. In other words, in considering the route, even before we have climbed on it, we invite a trojan horse into our mind. We do this with everything, however, with careers, money, status: outside of the values we attribute to them, they are meaningless. Life is value agnostic. Nietzsche, the great German thinker, was right on this point.

When we value things, we become attached to them, which invites anticipation, anxiety, desire, expectation, failure, self and, eventually, ego, but also, of course, elation, happiness, accomplishment ... all of which are perfectly normal, until you realize the trojan horse isn't doing you any good. Yet, a funny thing happens when you stop fetishizing the route—you just start *doing moves*. After much practice of just doing moves, you like climbing more, and you like it more often—and develop a deep sense of the craft of climbing. Here you get a glimpse of the eye of the *shokunin*. A radical form of embracing the process. Process is time without a goal: a hard unknown, not a soft unknown. Process is moment. Because your body is riveted in time, if we follow the cue of yoga, when we yoke ourselves to our spatio-temporal anchor, which is what a body really is, we, by a twist of mechanics, create the space for small mind to unmoor itself from distraction.

Jonathan Siegrist, one of the top sport climbers in the US, reiterates this near-universal formula for athletes wanting to do their best: "I think climbing your best is largely about quieting your mind enough to let your body do the work it's been trained to do. I pride myself on being somewhat of a master in this realm but there have also been times when it feels next to impossible. Ultimately, I only succeed when my focus is on the rock, the movement and the effort—and not on the outcome, consequences or my expectations."

As Irena Martinkova and Jim Parry put it in an article on Zen and sports, when movements are an end, rather than a means, our moves, and the athlete, become "instrumental." When that happens, quality degrades: A tennis player, for instance, only plays well enough to beat their opponent, or a climber climbs just well enough to get up a 5.9/5c when they are a 5.12a/7a+ climber (small experience). Both scenarios are unfortunate, not to mention missed opportunities for further perfecting the craft, since it would be wholly untrue to claim there's nothing to learn about climbing, and ourselves, when we are on easy terrain.

Since climbing is about routes and boulders and mountains, and routes are about moves, and moves are a body-in-performance, and performance is an experience, it follows that if you change the experience by removing the concept of the thing you are trying to achieve, you change your perception of the stone, and, with it, the nature of the climbing experience. It does not mean you have lost the fire to improve, only that improvement is redefined. You start to learn.

Doing Moves

Just to climb is something very few can do.

"When you eat, just eat. When you read the newspaper, just read the newspaper. Don't do anything other than what you are doing."
—*Seung Sahn, Korean Zen master*

This past spring, I decided to venture up a seldom-climbed 5.12c/7b+ at my local crag, called *The Puoux*, "conveniently" situated just above I70, the loud and obnoxious highway cutting through the heart of the Colorado mountains. The Puoux is a haven for bat colonies with a potentially deadly virus, beehives bigger than a grown adult, and chossy limestone, some of it drilled. But it's 25 minutes from my house, plus climbing above speeding traffic and trucks and horns is excellent Zen practice, like meditating in Times Square. Pristine is just a concept, anyway.

On my second burn on the route, after nearly getting the onsight, I found myself at a decent rest before a slight runout on a techy slab, two more bolts guarding the chains. At the rest, I was breathing and trying to recenter, but I was also starting to get pumped and couldn't quite settle, so I checked in with myself. What I found in my mind was hilarious: I was typing emails in my mind and going over conversations from work the previous afternoon. When I paid attention to this mind-stream, it was as if I was overhearing someone still working at their desk. Not even "as if." *I was.* I was on the climb, my muscles doing their thing, and I was also at a desk, rehashing work-related issues. Had I not thought to check in, I would have still done the climb, I think, but I would not have known why I was feeling unsettled. I would have enjoyed it less, that's for sure. I hung there on the jugs and started laughing at myself. As soon as I brought attention to the thoughts, they lost their power. Immediately, my body responded and started to regain its center, though not entirely, as you can only expect so much when you let your mind get to such a state. You have to be ok with mild improvement at that late of a stage.

There is a reason why one of the first things students of meditation learn is to keep their mind on their breath. Breath reconnects us to our body immediately, a simple and convenient source of focus that also serves to calm us down. It can take six to 12 months of daily practice to be mindful of your in-breath and out-breath for ten seconds. *Doing what you are doing* is much, much harder than you think. As Seung Sahn writes, "Don't do anything other than what you are doing." If you are breathing, breathe. If cooking rice, cook rice. If climbing, climb. The prescription, of course, applies to all moments in life.

Doing moves is the easiest thing to do and the most difficult for climbers. We climb in our bodies, and we only climb to our potential when we are in our body *to the fullest*. In philosophical and theoretical circles, it's called embodiment—the manner, method and means in which we become our bodies, tune in to them. Problems arise when we don't listen to our body, or we yell at it, or we try to hijack its intelligence by being a helicopter parent and hyper-controlling its movements. As if by a psychological law of entropy, it is when you remove intentionality that attachment, distraction and error fill the void. You become disembodied. An untended garden grows weeds. Why wouldn't it? A disembodied state allows attention to go elsewhere (the essence of disembodiment and small mind: being related to something outside itself) and this elsewhere germinates frustration, projection, performance anxiety, nervousness, ego, end-goal thinking, and so on. Leaving the climber with a feeling that they are not in control—on account of being enslaved to external factors—despite all efforts at control.

Children

The body craves attention. There is a primal joy in sensation that children know, but adults forget.

My wife is an art teacher, and she is astounded how kids go to the sink to wash paint from their hands, then spend 15 minutes playing with the water. Watching it pool, drizzle, and spiral down the drain. Filling things. Emptying things. Feeling it flow through their fingers. Water is amazing, really.

Children are enamored by everyday things because

they are present with them. But it's not just generic water: it's the *behavior* of water, its properties, how it reacts to objects, feels on our skin. The sensations are delightful. There is a magic in their world few have access to, which is also why the mindset of children has been considered a gold standard by philosophers and mystics for centuries. The cold sliminess of mud is a perverse pleasure. Water is amorphous, creative, an astonishment. Have the mind of a child, and the world is always new and interesting and engaging. Children don't judge. Remember the Garden of Eden—no self-awareness and no judgement. Children are seekers. Children feel directly and intensely: they have a germ of big mind, of a place adults need to return to in order to rediscover the world.

Adults grow up and stop looking: small mind. By default, the world loses its luster as a result of patterns in our mind that keep us from paying attention, but the fundamental magic of the world hasn't changed. We have just lost the ability to feel the world around us. I've been keenly aware of this adult-induced exile for a long time, and so I am constantly trying to reverse the trend, trying to see more, feel more, with varying amounts of success, however. But what that exercise has taught me is that the natural trajectory of life is often one of constriction of sensation, rather than opening of sensation. You have to fight the inertia of disembodiment and return to the wellspring of the body, which is stimulus. Climbing is one way, for us, to reverse the trend.

As children illustrate, the body craves single-pointed attention. The crude, primal joy in climbing is often just that: our fingertips caress, soak up data, learn how to interpret data, then send the data to our somatic architecture. Unsurprisingly, the fingertips, along with the tongue and lips, contain more nerve endings than other parts of the body, and, as research from *Nature Neuroscience* has discovered, our brains have actually outsourced some visual information processing tasks to our fingertips, enabling them to perform "neural computations," which means we are more like an octopus than we thought, the latter known for having mini-brains on the limbs of its body (in addition to a central brain).

Embodiment is thinking and the body is moving thought. Paying close attention to our bodies and the stone is like learning a new language. Learning a language is done by kids with a minimal amount of conscious effort. Why is it so hard for adults? Because we have a hyper-conscious approach to learning, because we get hang-ups, bring history to it, and get embarrassed. Because our neural patterns are more entrenched, forcing our minds into well-worn paths, as opposed to the neural plasticity of children. Kids absorb information differently—a large part of their (unconscious) absorption strategy is body-centered and stimulus-driven.

Doing moves is the fundamental language of climbing, except our language is more pictorial than grammatical, akin to the "rules" of abstract art. There are no rules, in fact, only compositions: those that work and those that don't. The compositions we put together should get us to the top. Those compositions should be part of a holistic collective, each enriching past and future works of art. Despite the talk of climbing being a sport of solving problems, we solve creative problems, not engineering problems. To solve creative problems, we need to learn and absorb information differently, with a free mind that is empowered to be creative, rather than a mind that holds itself back. We need to learn, or relearn, to be creative with the outside world.

Little Lies We Tell Ourselves

Trying something over and over again,
until exhaustion, is the easy part.

"On a personal level, pushing beyond your limits really comes down to the battle between the unconscious and conscious mind. You can rationalize and prove to your conscious part of the brain how you should be capable of something. And you can be genuinely convinced that you've got what it takes. But your subconscious mind may disagree. Your subconscious mind—in control of your survival instincts—has to be the realist."

Nalle Hukkataival, professional climber

The strongest pair of arms ever to hail from Finland—Hukkataival has bouldered V17/9a, *Burden of*

Dreams, one of just three of the grade globally, and as yet unrepeated. He spent years thinking and practicing the moves, but, as the quote above testifies, the hardest part wasn't the strength, but the internal battle, which sounds ridiculous, *because all you need to do is just drive to the boulder and try it, again and again, right?*

Wrong. Trying it over, again and again, is the easiest part.

When you fail for too long, doubt creeps in. You don't think it's possible. When a manager is building a young boxer, he is keen to get him fights he can win because losing in boxing is not like getting third in the track and field state finals. Sure, losing stings, but a boxer doesn't so much lose as *lose and get beat up*. Losing and getting beat up are often, though not always, the same thing in boxing. Doubt has a trickle-down effect on motivation, effort, intelligence applied, quality of effort and lost joy. The same rule applies for boxing as it does in climbing. Hukkataival isn't just talking about being confident. He is talking about looking deeply. He is talking about delusion. He is talking about gardening your mind. About sobering up. About aligning your subconscious with your conscious mind, which is technically impossible, because if something is subconscious it is by definition not conscious. Definitions aside, Hukkataival's observation is about truth-telling to oneself, about not telling yourself stories about yourself, stories that might be whispering success, all the while being told by someone who is insecure, and so needs the story as a buoy.

When projecting, you can go on doubting for a bit, but eventually, the doubt gets underlined and italicized in your mind, such that when you re-read a sequence in your thoughts, bad feelings start to accompany it. You know a bad feeling by what it is not: *not an inspiring feeling*. The relationship changes. As with all relationships, most tend not to stick around if it is all negativity and little joy. We pack up and leave, whether we have stayed there physically or not, because we can still be showing up to the crag and roping up, yet never really arriving. Doubt can be instrumental in counteracting overconfidence, but in this case, doubt is a force of stasis.

Eventually, if your project is miscalibrated, doubt settles into your subconscious, which then forms its own opinion on the viability of your success. And as Hukkataival knows, it's the subconscious voice you need to listen to, because this is the voice with the most influence. The subconscious can be just as wrong as your last-minute pep talk, but because it's unconscious, it's affecting you without you knowing it, like a weed growing in all directions. The voice with the most power is the one you're not aware of. Therein lies the danger.

Some walk away, but most stick around, and we start to drag our unwilling body to the crag. This is the earliest stage of "plateauing." You and your body lose motivation, which means your conscious mind will step in with pep talks and false claims of "having what it takes"—little lies we tell ourselves when things are desperate. The lies try to convince our subconscious, unsuccessfully. But our pep talks are surface medicine and cannot cure the virus. A pep talk is talking to a level of your psyche at the same level of doubt. You need to go deeper, to where the reasons for doubt first crept in. Likely, those reasons are entirely unrelated to climbing; the seeds of doubt originated elsewhere, either from experience at work or in bad relationships, or structural (how you depend on climbing to provide something it can't). Doubt and demotivation can also come from over-training or mental fatigue, both key examples of awareness errors. You need to address the subconscious part of your psyche, the *real* driver. Motivation, or lack thereof, does not originate in awareness, though awareness can often identify why we don't want to do something.

Doors of Perception

The ultimate religious experience is neither.

"'This is how one ought to see,' I kept saying as I looked down at my trousers, or glanced at the jeweled books in the shelves, at the legs of my infinitely more than Van-Goghian chair. 'This is how one ought to see, how things really are.' And yet there were reservations. For if one always saw like this, one would never want to do anything else."

Aldous Huxley, English writer and philosopher

Aldous Huxley's *The Doors of Perception*, from which Jim Morrison's *The Doors* got their name, was written under the influence of *Anhalonium lewinii*, a fancy name for Peyote. It's a great idea, kind of like Jack Kerouac cranking out *On the Road* and *Dharma Bums* while higher than a kite. Kerouac was a student of Zen, by the way. *The Doors of Perception* blew my mind when I read it. I felt like I was going on a trip with the author. I wanted to experience what he did. The book is about big mind, about what happens when your small mind starts to crack and the shell of its understanding—the concepts it creates around itself, to understand itself and the world—begin to peel away.

There's been an ongoing debate for thousands of years in religious mysticism about the *ultimate religious experience*. Christians have their version of mystical union with God, Jews their vision of aligning God, self and society, New Agers their desire for an undifferentiated oneness with the universe, Hinduism its union with Self, and so on. It has been a debate in my mind as well. Even after getting a PhD in the Philosophy of Religion, I found that none of the world's religions had a good answer, except Zen, at least to my mind. "At this very moment, what can be sought?" wrote Hakuin Ekaku, a Zen teacher of the 18th century. "Nirvana is immediate. This place is the lotus body. This body is the buddha body." That cryptic statement, of finding the mystical in the ordinary, seduced and fascinated me. I was obsessed. It took me decades to understand what it meant.

For the Zen masters, the profound was right in front of you, the *most* ordinary. You didn't have to go through special ceremonies, you didn't have to learn a book for thirty years. But that moment isn't waiting for us to pick it up. It takes a lot of *work* to get *here*. Some sports thrust you into that *work*, while others might require more attention. Since the stakes are so high in climbing, often embodying life or death situations, climbers are in a unique position to go low on the brain stem and explore the subconscious material bubbling up when we are staring down at, for instance, a broken back with one slip of the foot. Unlike football or rugby, climbing has a unique way of letting us explore the constellation of the present, because the latter isn't one thing.

My first real memory of climbing was doing the *Ruper* in Eldorado Canyon, a classic six-pitch 5.8/5b on the Front Range of Colorado. After climbing for only a year or so, I had never really led anything. I was wearing a *No Fear* shirt and gray sweatpants, if that tells you anything. My shoes were a size too big. It was a hot and humid summer day, and when it's hot, Eldo loses its friction, and the rock feels super-polished. I forget what pitch, but I took the lead, immediately got off route, and while standing there on bad feet with my last piece of shit protection 20 feet below me, my webbing harness fell to my feet. Because, of course, I had forgotten my harness that day. We had fashioned one in the parking lot at the last minute, and now, at this moment, the harness had enough of me.

It was the first time in my life when I saw myself dying. It wasn't a heavy or cumbersome thought but a vision of careening onto the sloping ledge, then bouncing to the base of the cliff. I saw my body go limp. I saw my bones break. I saw myself losing consciousness rather quickly after I'd hit the first ledge. It sounds morbid but wasn't, more like, "Huh, so that's how it goes." The thought came naturally, and I didn't stop it. My pulse did start racing, and my hands, already sweaty, felt dipped in butter. My thoughts started to get the best of me. I yelled down. My partners were out of range and could hear nothing. I was alone. No one could help me. What had to be done was very clear, and I realized then and there I couldn't do what I needed to do with my mind in that state. So, I told it to shut the hell up and let me get on.

After a few minutes, I down-climbed, traversed back right, and yelled down, asking for help. I found my way to the top of the pitch, and rather than turning me off climbing, it turned me on, not because of the risk factor, or the allure of self-reliance, but because of the places it forced my mind to go, places it hadn't gone before. Places it is hard to go otherwise. In short, that is *the ask*. It was my first real Zen experience, when all of my past intersected with the present, when I had seen very clearly, if momentarily, the bones of what awareness exhumes. A window had been opened courtesy of *the ask*. My small mind had formed a crack.

Death Cards

*Feeling the brevity of life has a counterintuitive
and liberating effect of making it longer.*

Almost three decades later, after the moment when
my harness fell to my feet, *the ask* comes to me on
a monthly basis. I still look down and can't help but
wonder what would happen if I fall.

~ *I see my body ricocheting down.*
~ *I see the light in my mind going black.*
~ *I tell my family I love them.*
~ *I see my family missing me.*

I rivet my attention to each move of my finger,
each swing of my ice tool.

It's not heroic. It's what we do.

It could be argued that allowing these thoughts to
enter my mind in such a precarious position is the mark
of a distracted, uncentered mind, and that rather than
let them in, I need to build up the defenses to keep
them out. The thoughts are unnecessary, and very
un-Zen. That could be so. But it's hard to argue this
visual imagery isn't the most natural thought to have.

A body senses its mortality whether you want to
acknowledge it or not. More often than not, allowing these thoughts to come to the forefront of my
mind, giving them space to settle in, has the opposite
effect of ignoring them. When you repress them, you
give them license to wreak havoc behind the scenes.
Untended thoughts become panic because panic

is undisciplined thought. But when you give them prime real estate, give them a seat at the table, they lose their power and stop acting like petulant children. Coming to terms with these thoughts doesn't make you risk-averse, just risk-conscious. These thoughts provide data. Information. You might not like the information, but that's another matter. Of course, it's fluid. You can't think of the people you love the *moment* you make a risky move, as that would be *unskillful means*, but you need to at the appropriate time. Being risk-conscious helps you make better decisions in risky situations. Allowing the body to communicate risk without fear or censorship generates a communication pattern, and internal culture, where you legitimate the body's concerns, which serves as a beacon constantly reminding you when you're in a tight spot. If you have a clear mind, it will never be wrong. It will not over- or underreact. Fear overreacts when it doesn't have a microphone. Having written dozens of reports on deaths and accidents for climbing magazines, I can say that a large number of them are from either not knowing the real gravity of a situation, and/or becoming complacent. Both are errors of awareness. Becoming *more* conscious is the point of meditation. Becoming risk-conscious is just doing the *more* in climbing.

Throughout history, Buddhist, Hindu, and Christian monks have long practiced forms of death meditation. Some monks in Thailand carry around images of corpses to be constantly reminded of the impermanence of life. Christians, for their part, have a dying body at the center of their system. Hindus burn bodies by the Ganges, and many sects of Indian masters live in graveyards and rub the ash of dead bodies on their skin. Some Tibetans chop up the bodies of deceased, called a sky burial, and leave the body parts for the animals. Despite vastly different contexts, the impulse is the same—the flush of mortality is a powerful antidote to the ruts life builds in our (small) minds. Like those children playing with water for twenty minutes, *the ask* forces us to pay attention, like a child, to the materiality, and mutability, of life.

Religious and philosophical systems have the means, and methods, to incorporate death meditation into a holistic framework. There, it is encouraged, makes sense, and doesn't traumatize. In contrast, climbers typically have the near-death experience and lack the training to bring that experience into the deeper folds of our lives (integration). Actually, most of the time climbers repress the thoughts, because that makes us feel vulnerable, and when you are vulnerable, you hesitate. And a climber can't hesitate in the mountains. But this is the heart of embodiment—integrating bodily experience back into our body–mind, which sounds like something that should be automatic, except it isn't. We constantly block the channels of integration with pride, fear of appearing weak, ego, fear of losing control, and so on. We do it in climbing to the extent we do it in life. If we are insecure in our relationships, we will be so in climbing.

Climbing underscores the fragility of existence and tells us how we mask that fragility with mental habitude—civilization creates a "safe" existence, but it's a ruse. What climbing does is simply remove those blinders through the act of climbing, and, ideally, we can carry over the experience to life and living. Knowing, seeing, understanding and feeling the brevity of life has the counterintuitive but liberating effect of teaching us how to live. It helps us cultivate the art of living, moment by moment, which is big mind. Like Jim Dine's students erasing their drawings at the end of each day, we become art students in life.

Geworfenheit

*Complacency dims the mind and
the experiences of it.*

That day, in Eldorado, when I was young and on the sharp end, and my harness fell to my ankles, *the ask* told me, right then and there, that I was in control of my fate, that things, bad things, arrive in your life without you asking, but that you have to do something about them. Experience is malleable. Existence is impermanent. The moment was asking me, *what are you going to do with your life?*

Martin Heidegger, a German philosopher of the first half of the 20th century, wrote at length of *geworfenheit*, or "thrownness." Existence itself, for Heidegger, is characterized by being born into a family, nation, town, culture, etc., without any say in the matter. We are simply thrown into existence and asked to make sense of it. We have been dropped here. We are essentially without "home," and the lack of a home manifests in various ways.

If our alienated homelessness is existential anxiety writ large, writ small it is *the ask*. Few sports do this. It's not an ideal scenario to push yourself so far, but it's a reality and attraction in climbing. It's not a secret that many climbers use the climbing experience as sushi lovers use ginger—to clear the palette before the next round, to hit reset, rearrange priorities. Figure out what is real. Pull out the invasive species. The invasive species isn't a sense of mortality, per se, it is complacency, the small mind, which masks the true nature of existence. When we are complacent, we let our guard down. The colors dim. Experiences dim. We stop being a gardener of our inner experience. We allow invasive species to flourish, choking sunlight. *The ask* is a re-enactment of being born, a primal confrontation with *geworfenheit,* and climbing is a super-facilitator for the question.

Mental Ecosystems

*Nerves are the most common invasive species
in the climber's mind.*

Mental ecosystems work in the same manner as invasive species: some emotions, concepts, ideas, reactions, or thoughts are invasive. Invasive species don't belong in our ecosystems natively, which isn't to say these species are good or bad in essence (dualism is a myth), only good or bad *as regards* performance and potentiality in specific ecosystems (ours, the climbing one). They are part of life like anything else. We can pretend to remove all end-goal thinking from our own motivations, but we can't from climbing. There is no such thing as an activity without value. Even sitting on a meditation mat, with a clear mind, your heart is beating and your lungs are expanding and contracting. Your body is keeping you alive so that you can pass on your DNA. Everything has a *telos*. Climbing requires we move up something. Remove that end, and we are not talking about climbing. The point isn't to engage in activities without value, but rather to see the values, aka mental ecosystems, we bring to activities. We do this to gain control over ourselves, and to be more creative in life.

Our ecosystems are like a field we have been consciously and unconsciously cultivating from birth. On this field are paths, habit trails, cairns, ruts and places we never go, metaphorically speaking. Some people allow anxiety a parcel in their ecosystem and have for years. They are ok with it; they unconsciously encourage it. They water their anxiety with comforting self-talk and self-forgiveness. And when they look inside and see it, they shouldn't blame anxiety for being there. The simple fact that it's there is because their ecosystem is ideal for its growth—just the right amount of insecurity, fear of the unknown and past experiences to justify the anxiety. There, in their mind, it found moist soil, sunshine and no gardener to pluck it out. So, like any life form, it grows.

For climbers and athletes, the obvious question is—what are the mental ecosystems occluding top performance? What are the most common invasive species in the athlete's mind? For climbers, nerves are the predominant invasive species, manifesting in nervousness, beta-botching, fear of falling, doubt, trying too hard or trying too little. For a good part of my climbing life, I too had told myself a story about nerves, a story that allowed them to grow and thrive in the recesses of my mind. But while stories are entertaining, they mask.

Nerves Like Ghosts

Nerves can't be calmed rationally because their manifestation is typically not the result of a failure of rationality.

Nerves. They show up everywhere in climbing like phantom ghosts, arriving in our tents in the winter before a hard alpine climb, suddenly on a hard lead above a tipped-out cam, or the morning of the last day of a trip, and we know the weather is about to turn shit, and this is it, we must do it today ... or the next go.

Climbing acts on the nervous system in a way javelin or curling or the high jump cannot. It's not about sports being superior; they're just different. Death inhabits our sport at a deep level (*the ask*), even if we have no conscious awareness of dying. It's like hesitating to pick up an entirely harmless six foot black snake. My body reacts, recoils, despite knowing consciously that it's not going to strangle me. Why? Evolutionary biologists tell us a fear of snakes is a reaction deep into our neural-mind complex, for a good reason. Early humans had good reason to fear snakes … just as modern humans have good reason to fear being stranded on a cliff. It takes repeated experience with snakes to overcome our primal fear, but this does not mean it still doesn't exist on a deeper neurological level. It does. In fact, all the talk of climbing, big wave surfing or base jumping making us feel "more alive" on account of us being closer to death testifies to the peculiar psychosomatic energies provided by them. Nerves, at least the type born of mortality, are the body pinging us with crucial information, mortal danger being just a slice of the data set.

Eventually, if you do the work long enough, you won't have to deal with nerves so much. As American Olympic silver medalist Nathaniel Coleman observed: "When a competition is going well, I think I'm just relaxing into a bath of positive emotions. And that's not something I have to focus on trying to do. It's something that just happens."

However, getting there is difficult, like telling someone just to love the process or be in the moment. It doesn't work like that. And it never works quickly.

You can't say, "Nerves … just chill," because they don't operate at a linguistic or a rational level. They can't be calmed rationally because their existence is typically not the result of a failure of rationality. You can't tell a jealous boyfriend to stop being jealous and expect it to work, *just like that*. The person needs to do real work on the roots of their jealousy, the causes, the origins, the history, and that trip will undoubtedly take them places they haven't been before. It just *happens* for Coleman because he has done the work, and yes, your biological constitution can help or hinder your progress, but it is not determinative. A big mind attuned to the small mind is the only cure, a cure with no essential dependency on biological constitution.

Neural Pathways

Small mind doesn't heal small mind.
Big mind can't be corrupted.

Technically speaking, climbing movement could be compared to standing on one leg and juggling, or running at a decent pace while doing math problems in your head. The stuff we do has a brute physical component, requiring precision, timing, grace at times, but it is also calculative and analytical. If I were to ask you to do *one* of these things, you'd have fun doing it. You wouldn't get nervy. Why is that?

It's all in what you are adding to your climbing. To eradicate mental performance nerves, you have to change neural pathways. For nearly all deep-seated mental afflictions, you need to go "lower" than the affliction, which is why many smokers, or sufferers of chronic depression, have turned to magic mushrooms, Ayahuasca (yage), or other varieties of non-traditional medicine to help them quit smoking. The recontextualization of your life is the best medicine and longest-lasting form of healing. Hallucinogens provide that new context via various out-of-mind or out-of-body experiences, and they rewire your brain because they lead you to think about life differently. Fundamentally, they can change the way you think, and that alteration has a trickle-down effect. Small mind doesn't heal small mind—only big mind can do that.

Rewiring your mind, for example, not to crave cigarettes when you are bored, is extremely difficult and no light matter. The point is, if you suffer from perennial anxiety, it will not be solved with self-help-style pep talks two minutes before you tie in, which is what most climbers do. That is like preparing for the flood with a bucket beneath the dam. The bucket will work for a bit and you can go through life like this, but it's rather exhausting. This is because your nerves are reacting to something very real and tangible to your organism—fear of injury, fear of failure, a knock to your self-worth, embarrassment, pressure for recognition, etc. This goes for all forms of anxiety we experience on a daily basis. Nerves are a form of information, and the biggest problem is we don't have tools to interpret the data, and/or we think such information is mere noise.

Non-Dualism

*Nerves are often the result of things
we place between movement and its execution.*

All those things we bring to a climb, all the things we rely on climbing to provide us—self-worth, accomplishment, etc.—can cause nerves for the simple fact that what is at stake in the performance is no longer just the act of performing, but rather what happens *after* the fact. What happens *after* is a result of the meaning we give (attach) to a climb. Like the previous juggling example ... you wouldn't attach meaning to your failure, or success, at your inability to run a 1:15 lap around the track while doing multiplication problems. Why would you? You are not emotionally invested in it. You don't care. *But, I want to climb hard,* you say. *I am passionate about it. I want to get better. If I lose sight of these goals, it's just blah and I'm just climbing with no goal or focus. I won't improve.* Nothing is further from the truth. It is only in letting go that we find anything in its truest state, which applies equally to athletic motivation and friends, for example. Retain the goals but toss the dishonest reasons for wanting to achieve them. Once you sober up and see these ugly thoughts rear their heads, they will hold less power over you.

The meanings we attach to a climb are not part of the climbing experience. The meanings are second-tier abstractions, akin to the way we look at a drooping willow tree and feel sadness. The tree isn't sad. We are projecting. Our emotions are abstractions, interpretations, taken from our mental ecosystems and guided by the tree's physicality. Concepts are abstractions as well. Success, or failure, is a second-tier abstraction we layer over the climbing experience. In reality, there is no more success in climbing to the top of a route than there is in a boulder rolling down a hill. The boulder does not get to the bottom and think, "I did it!! Hell yeah!" The natural world is valueless, value-defined, in its most basic form, as the designation of good or bad. Consciousness adds value. Matter was moved across time and space in the case of the boulder and the climber, that is all. That matter is conceptually agnostic and unthinking, that is, until consciousness intervenes and generates abstractions. These abstractions become attachments when they feel "sticky" to us, when we allow them a place in our mental ecosystem. They are attachments when we hold onto them and allow them to interpret an experience (which renders it small), as opposed to being nonjudgemental as to what arrives, what is *to come*, from an experience (big experience).

Some attachments you can see clearly, and so let them go. When you can see them clearly, their force is minimized, they lose their grip, the mechanism being that, when it can, ignorance is a fine and "natural" leader. At other times the abstractions exert great force, to the extent you have no control or are unaware of their provenance. When Zen talks about extinguishing small mind so we can experience a state of non-dualism, it is in part talking about removing concepts (specific values) from our experience, because like attachments, concepts are ugly intermediaries living between us and a "deeper" experience. Concepts create dualism, and the *heart of dualism is valuation*: this is good, this is bad. This is that, this is not that. I am good, I am bad. I am climbing bad, I am climbing good. I'm unhappy that I'm climbing bad. I'm happy that I'm climbing good. From one valuation, *I'm climbing good*, the kinetic chain strengthens to *I am such and such*, then it gathers complexity, such as the sense of not trusting ourself when we are not climbing good, which leads to nervousness and feeling unsuited to the task. It's a problem because each valuation in this chain can be inaccurate. But it can also be accurate. Your body can be having an off day, and so, if you can see that clearly, you shouldn't try that dangerous 5.12 runout. Of course, you have to make conscious decisions based on analysis, but decisions—especially those that involve risk—need to be anchored in a clear mind, not a clouded one. The downstream effects of this cycle are profound— weeds sprout in our minds in various directions.

Cycle of Self-Criticism

Internal dialogue, whether positive or negative,
is negative.

In *The Inner Game of Tennis*, Timothy Gallwey defines the typical athlete's inner world as Self 1 and Self 2. Simplified to an old dualism, Self 1 is the mind, and Self 2 is the body. This internal split is not ideal, because in an ideal scenario the body–mind interface is smooth, glitch-free and transparent. Gallwey's ideas, however, are helpful because they shed a light on a common symptom of attachments—internal dialogue.

A former player and coach, and someone well trained in meditation, Gallwey found the following structure in the mental game of hundreds of athletes: Self 1 judges Self 2 when a mistake is made.

You idiot, you knew to grab the hold differently.

You knew better.

What were you thinking?

We say these things to ourselves when we make mistakes. We get angry with our bodies. With parts of ourselves, say the part of ourselves that hesitates. We hold grudges against it, and it takes us a while for us to forgive it. Therefore, the cycle of self-criticism, body valuations, and mistrust begins.

Gallwey writes about trying to uncouple bad actions with bad valuations, such as when we botch a move on a climb, we judge it as the wrong move, and therefore, we chastise our body for making the wrong move. *We* become bad. But "wrong" moves only exist as judgements (concepts) in relation to a goal—movement *just is*. Movement is not good or bad. Yet, there is effective and ineffective movement, according to the rules of the climbing game. But, while ineffective movement does have executionary valuation, it is without conceptual, and therefore emotional, valuation. For instance, you have to acknowledge that getting the sloper with your left hand is better than your right, but you have to stem the tide of creeping valuations, including the possibility of failure, or success.

When I walk down the street, nothing pops in my head that says, *You idiot, why did you walk that way?* I'm just walking. It's not a game. But since athletics needs to give valuation to movement, because it is task and goal-oriented, it opens the door to valuations about *who* is doing the executing and *who* is the cause of bad execution. But it's false conflation when a move is seen as "wrong": it does not mean the person doing it is wrong. It simply means there is a better way of doing it or that a mistake was made. To chastise the body for not doing it right is surely one of the most ineffective strategies in learning. The body is going to make mistakes, period. Self-chastising sows the seeds of disunion, and later, internal rebellion, such as fragmentation, which eventually produces the parts of us we don't like, but seem to not be able to control. We don't control them because we don't listen to them, don't understand them; hence the importance of compassion and kindness to oneself. If you need to chastise anything, it is the voice that is doing the chastising because you have misaligned expectations, or you have not given your body the proper resources to execute the sequence.

When movement is end-oriented, you open the door to self-judgement, and self-judgement almost always comes with emotion attached. Rudolf Tefelner, one of Adam Ondra's mentors, writes: "Impact of emotions on performance? It's negative even with positive emotions. If you're without emotions, only focusing without any thoughts, any emotions, then you can give it all you have. And you'll enjoy it later." Or, as Patrick Mouratoglou, former coach of Serena Williams, says, "Emotions are the worst advisor."

Mind-streams

*The mind tends to think it has no limitations,
while the body is the opposite.*

Nerves are activated when the body senses it has lost control. It's not fair to put so much pressure on the body. The body has real limitations of tendon strength, fitness, muscular contraction, and so on, while it is a property (or delusion) of the mind that it can transcend space and limits—a type of thinking that tries to direct performance: "I can do anything." No, you can't. "Doing anything" means nothing. The continued pressure on the body will only sour the relationship further, and it will fight back and spoil your performance. Nerves are symptomatic of that rebellion. Nerves are self-sabotage.

Mind-streams are threads of our consciousness looking for integration into the rest of our being, and it's dangerous when mind-streams start to get attached to outcomes. Typically, we label mind-streams distractions, but distraction is also a form of information. Meditation, or active awareness, is the act of turning mind-streams into information. If you are distracted because your mind keeps replaying a hurtful conversation, it means there is unfinished business. The existence of the distraction is telling. Some mind-streams go rogue because, at the highest level, they are artificial and impossible to integrate.

For instance, many people say they are climbers. Climbing defines them. I've said this all my life, as my life, and now my professional life, revolves around climbing. Four to five times a week, I'm climbing something—ice, rock, walls, cracks, mountains. All my friends and family know me as a climber, and nearly all my friends are climbers. But I'm a climber, and I'm not a climber. Climbing suits me. I am configured to it historically and bodily. But I'm also aware that identifying as "being an x" can often rob the joy of it. We feel obliged to indulge it. We take fewer breaks from it because, as a climber, we feel we wouldn't be one if we didn't want to climb—that's called imposter syndrome. We feign motivation, then we force it, then lose motivation and get burnt out. We are worried one day we will wake up and not like climbing, and that's scary, so we grasp tighter. The joy in it dampens. Careers are no different. We treat loved ones with the same suffocating embrace. We grasp out of fear.

Climbing had made *the ask* of me, and I answered each time, wilfully. But for a long section of my climbing career, I was not *doing moves*. I wasn't present with it. I was bringing too much to the crag, and it weighed me down. I had thought perfection was to be found in continuing to load climbing with the things it couldn't provide—adventure, sense of self, uniqueness—and then calibrating my climbing so this projection of perfection would be achieved. Perfection was, on this account, about having my climbing goals align with my life goals, and I leaned on climbing like a crutch to help me achieve those goals. Improvements in my climbing meant self-improvement. I thought climbing my first 5.14/8b+, M11 or V11/8a would give me something lasting, but it turns out I was wrong on what climbing was and who I was.

After climbing for almost 30 years, I asked myself why I liked to climb. Then I made myself a promise, telling myself it is with climbing as it is with writing—I will walk away the second I don't want to do it. Luckily, I wake up every day wanting to climb and write, and I give this perennial motivation credit partly because I expect nothing from it, and partly because I have no fear of falling out of love with it, a fear causing most people to choke the very things they love.

Self and Sport

The body doesn't need an operator.
It will operate by itself.

Some of the earliest Christian monastics were considered "athletes of God." They would do mind-blowing things assuming that they would be brought closer to God. They would fast for weeks, live in caves, stand on narrow pillars, like ancient David Blaine in the desert. Much like Hindu *sadhus*, they used their bodies as their means to reach the spiritual. But most essentially, the monastics attempted to purify their souls by *first* purifying their will, which was considered to be the deep driver of conscious decision making. For years the monks would pray, but they found that purifying the will was extremely difficult, to the point that sinful thoughts would still steal upon their minds even after decades of rigorous discipline. They got frustrated. They fasted longer, to the point of death. They secluded themselves with greater severity. Most concluded, rightfully, that sinful thought could never entirely be erased. Even the greatest saints still found themselves riveted to "fleshly desire," "passions," and the vicissitudes of their minds. What they found they *could* achieve was dampening the force those thoughts had in acting upon their will. With big mind, small mind isn't erased, but it comes into focus and loses its grip on your existence.

Buddhists would agree—you can't so much change the thoughts you have as much as weaken or diminish their power. In time, through diligence and awareness, the noise decreases in volume. But rewiring our will is a fool's errand. The will, the seat of decision making, is nothing but an ethically renamed ego, which, to a Buddhist, doesn't exist anyway. It manifests, but it has no stable core and is in a constant state of change. It's an illusion. A hungry ghost. Changing our thought is difficult because it is the nature of mind to be reactionary. Athletes are in an analogous situation. We are trying to purify our will, so that our bodies do what we want them to do. But we have it backwards. The body doesn't need to be whipped; it will operate by itself. It doesn't need a will to believe. To let the body be a body, for starters, you need to repair the relationship you have with it.

One of the most relied-upon tools for the athletic mindset has been belief. "I believe I can do it." "I believe in myself." All our lives we are told to never lose faith, never lose your belief that such and such is possible. But what if, in the very mechanics of belief, we were to find the construction of an architecture of failure?

Belief

Believing in oneself is like stuffing a jacket into the hull of a sinking ship.

Belief is a multi-layered cake. There is committing to a long-term project and believing you can do it. There is committing to training and believing it will make you a stronger climber. There is a state of being doubtful before a redpoint burn and telling yourself to shut up, that *you can do it. You just need to believe in yourself.*

According to the *Oxford English Dictionary*, belief is "an opinion about something; something that you think is true," or "a strong feeling that something or someone exists or is true; confidence that something or someone is good or right." In other words, it's an opinion, a strong feeling of confidence in something or someone. Typically, we attribute belief to a voice inside us—the one that says *keep going*. Belief is one of our better angels, yet it's a rogue thread in our consciousness, which, despite all the negative things I'm going to say about belief, does serve a function in some scenarios.

Belief operates between two realities—the one you *are* in and the one you *want* to be in. Belief works with unknowns, and is, as a result, forward facing. The reality is: you are about to try something, and you believe that you can finish it. It's a hard boulder problem, or a hard route. It's hard for you. You don't think you can do it, so belief steps in. You think this belief, this opinion—because belief *is an opinion, a wager*—will make you try harder. You think believing is essential ... because without belief there is negativity, right? Opposite belief is debilitating doubt? Not so. If I am good at golf, I can still swing a golf club even though I might not believe I can. I can spend an entire day convincing myself I can't swing a club, but, sure enough, when I step up to the green and swing, my body does it. You can *not try*, and you *can* self-sabotage, but that isn't related to belief. The body doesn't really care what your mindstream *believes*. Belief bolsters a fragile ego, and it is additive, rather than subtractive, which means it is an additional layer of valuation between you and doing moves. The body is remarkable at doing what it knows how to do. Belief is needed when you don't know, which means you are out of touch with what you do know.

Commandments of Athletic Effort

Perfection means "to finish."
But what, exactly, is being finished?

Western athletics has promoted a story we tell ourselves. This story is activated in just about every sport we play, from soccer to hockey to the marathon to climbing. It is *in* the Olympic story, and perhaps *is* the Olympic story: athletes transcending their limitations, willing themselves beyond themselves. The Olympic motto is *Citius, altius, fortius*. Faster, higher, stronger. They are the commandments of athletic effort:

1. Inside me, I've got a will.
2. My will is the engine of effort.
3. I need to activate the will to go faster, higher, stronger.
4. The will is needed to activate the essence of ourselves.
5. When the will is activated, the body listens.
6. Without great efforts of the will, athletic performance cannot reach its full potential.
7. There is value in overcoming, in transcending the body.
8. When we do so we encounter our real selves, despite the glaring contradiction of overcoming *and* finding at the same time.

These principles are also those of the hero of literature and adventure epics. It's romantic. It's idealistic. When the Olympics began in ancient Greece in the 7th-century BCE, to honor the god Zeus and for city-states to compete against one another, athletes fit the mold of existing archetypes: superhumans who did not tire like the rest of us. Whereas we get tired and quit, Olympians, like the gods, keep going, keep pushing. In part, this is why Greek gods were so muscular, because muscle and the ability to not get tired were paired.

The Olympic formula, essential to its own mythos, seems so tried and true that countering it would be like contradicting gravity.

Of course, you need to believe in yourself.
Of course you have a will.
Of course you need to overcome yourself.
Of course you need to transcend your body.

But what if belief, like confidence, is overvalued? What if "believing you will have a perfect performance" is the dominant cause of you *not* having one?

The concept of perfection comes from the Latin *perficio*, which doesn't have connotations of excellence, but rather, completion: *to finish*. A "perfect" expedition is when you summit a mountain. A "perfect" onsight is when you clip the chains. The question we need to ask is: what does it mean to "finish?" Is "to finish" closing something, or opening something? If it is opening, to what is it opening? If closing, who or what is being closed out? In terms of experience, because that is what a route *is*, what would completing an experience mean?

Can an experience ever be completed, or opened? No, it can't. Experience is the great "Heraclitus stream"—the one that changes every time we step into it. Small mind closes experience, and thinks it is a possession, but big mind sees the interconnectivity and the constant tide. Small mind is a small part of big experience.

What, then, is perfection?

It is human artifice to think one experience stops and another begins, or that quality of experience can be compartmentalized or aligned to this or that event, person, place or thing. Such thinking is the source of many problems. Before climbing and after climbing, experience keeps going. It's all a flow from the day we are born. Believing you can capture experience has led to the false notion of bottling performance after it is done, either in the form of success or failure.

Failure

Failure occurs in small mind.
Have goals, just no end posts.

"The biggest challenge probably to send a hard route is to not lose your mind or freak out on your way to climbing it, because dealing with failure or not succeeding all the time, for a long period of time, kind of gets you."
– *Alex Megos, professional German climber*

Around my hometown of Carbondale, Colorado, I've got ten times more projects I haven't done than the ones I have. That means failure is always around me, each time I go climbing. They stare at me, draws hanging, as I drive or walk past. Day and night, at work and in the shower, I visualize myself climbing on them, pulling through the crux, then failing. But I have learned that if I climb them well each time and still don't do them, the time clearly hasn't come yet. I've learned to develop patience, and I don't see failure anymore. What I see is the anxiety, the anticipation, and then I release it. I see an opportunity to climb without mistakes. In place of bitterness and ravenous desire—*arrggh,* those hungry ghosts—I have found opportunities for learning, which is what you so often fail to do when you are rushing to "complete" something. There is still a thing in me that looks like desire, but it isn't desire. I'm not filling a gap. I'm not deluding myself. I have goals, but no end posts. Not doing these routes does not sting, since doing them or not is unmoored from a sense of self. There's no "I" that cares if I did them or not, but this does not mean I lose motivation to climb. Rather, climbing is the joy, and that was lost to me for years. It is lost to a lot of climbers.

As a civilization, we have put a human on the moon and identified the parts of nanoparticles. We have developed ways to scan hundreds of feet into solid bedrock and can send waves of energy back and forth to space at such a speed that we can talk on the phone and not even know what's actually happening … but failure … we still don't understand that. But it doesn't have to be this way. It is possible to never feel like a failure again.

We don't understand the causes of failure because they are so nuanced, so multifaceted. Rather, as athletes, we have subsets of failure, like being "off our center," or "getting the yips," or "choking under pressure," which, according to researchers in a 2015 paper in *Frontiers in Behavioral Neuroscience*, is "not well understood yet." Or, as is stated in another paper in the *Journal of Experimental Psychology*, "Nevertheless, the phenomenon of 'choking under pressure' remains unexplained—and feared—by skilled performers across many domains." In each paper, however, the cause of choking is attributed to lack of attention due to distraction, or misaligned awareness and self-consciousness. Choking need not have a *universal* explanation, but it does have an explanation. The problem is just that the explanation is intensely individual, the only solution coming from an awareness of why one is distracted. Not just distracted by a noise in the stands, but inwardly distracted, distracted as fragmented. Distracted from purpose. To remove distraction, you need to unshackle yourself from small mind.

When you feel failure, the world changes. The trees outside your window are less bright. The fall winds don't inspire. Your energy levels decrease. Constant failure leads to depression. Failure for athletes is very destructive. We lose motivation. We start to fear performing. We lose hope. And yet, some athletes are entirely motivated by the fear of failure, or of losing.

In *The Weight of Gold*, Olympic gold medalist Apollo Ohno doesn't mince his words: "Most of my career I was driven purely by a fear of failure." Ohno isn't alone in the sporting world of high-end competition. One could say that the fear of failure served him well, given his eight Olympic medals. So what's the problem? The problem was he wasn't happy. He knew it wasn't a pure source of motivation, that it was an impure source of drive. Unsustainable. Fear makes you run, and Ohno was running. Ohno, like Michael Phelps, was driven by the wrong thing for so long that he is now dealing with the after-effects: depression.

Failure is premised on the notion of disappointment, or at least the feeling of failure is. Because it's a concept, a valuation: failure occurs in small mind. It is the feeling of failure that is the same as feeling *like* a failure. We don't feel like a failure if we are shooting some hoops with friends at the park and not keeping score, and we line it up for a three-pointer and whiff it. Who cares. We don't feel like a failure because it doesn't matter. We are not emotionally invested in either the outcome or the act.

The intensity of the feeling of failure arrives in proportion to the amount of libido you put into something. Failure is a simple mechanical error and entirely natural—you missed a hold, etc—but *feeling like a failure* is an error of attachment and the valuations you place upon movement, or yourself. Now, many will say, not being attached to an outcome is easy if you're an amateur and don't depend on winning to support yourself. That's true, to a point, but that is normalizing dysfunction, and, as all top athletes know, if you want to perform well with regularity, choose the sustainable strategy. If you remove emotional investment in an outcome, you don't feel like a failure when the outcome doesn't arise. Big mind absorbs the mistake, sees it for what it is, sees the small mind react to it with petty ego-driven reactions. Big mind should laugh at small mind's failures because the very concept of an outcome, while still contained within big mind (everything is), is a perversion of our basic nature. Basic nature is the same as big experience. Feeling like an athletic failure is a double sin: you have attached a false evaluation to a mirage.

Anxiety

Athletes who perform under pressure don't feel pressure but change the nature of pressure.

"When we worry that bad things might happen to us we are actually rehearsing them. We are building new neural pathways toward failure."

Lanny Bassham, Olympic Gold medalist, writer

According to the American Psychological Association (APA), anxiety is "an emotion characterized by feelings of tension, worried thoughts and physical changes like increased blood pressure." Other definitions define anxiety as the *sensation of experiencing failure in advance*, a way your body *lives* a future failure in the present. For athletes, anxiety gets thrown into the bag with fear of failure. Belief, which could be said to be an emotion characterized by feelings of success in advance, and anxiety share the same structure, but with a different end. In many ways, belief tries to smother anxiety, or at least keep it in check.

Unchecked, anxiety leads to crippling doubt, a hyperconscious and judging mind, stiffness in body, misaligned awareness, negative self-talk, and so on. Small mind becomes smaller. In contrast, athletes who perform well under pressure do not actually perform *under* pressure. Rather, the pressure forces them into a singular focus that *allows* that pressure to morph into pure, undistracted execution. They can climb with clarity. All forms of mental disharmony contort the body. In athletics, this symptom-manifestation cycle is even more pronounced. Regret, feeling you have failed, is typically the result.

Anticipation, defined as giving advance thought to something, is not the same as anxiety, though you can't have the latter without the former. Anticipation can be beneficial. Visualization is a form of anticipation. Creative imagination is a form of anticipation. Decision making requires anticipation. Many athletes resort to ritual to combat anxiety, to keep their thoughts on familiarity and repeatable habit patterns. Any novel introductions to this focus process can instill anxiety if these methods are untested. The question you need to ask yourself is: what exactly are you anticipating?

To anticipate, however, is also to think about something *to come*, and in this sense, it is a fundamental process of predictive and analytical thinking. You certainly can't move around in life or climb without thinking of what is to come. You can't go in "blind."

When you are looking at a boulder and feeling your forearms, and gauging how long to rest, you need to anticipate how you feel against what is required. When you are mid-route and shaking out at a jug, you need to anticipate what comes next. At other times, you need to have a beta-sequence running in the background of your mind, with just enough intensity that your memory feeds your psychosomatic streams with the right information, but not too much intensity such that you are so beholden to the sequence you can't adjust for variables. The trick is not trying to shut down the mind's processes ("no-mind" isn't feasible), but rather toggling freely between intensities of psychosomatic-informed mind-streams (body-informed data). Being free and not getting stuck is the goal. The mind isn't a light switch with a binary on or off position. No hard and fast dualities can be found here. It is more like a wave-pool or bar graph characterized by what French philosopher Gilles Deleuze called *multiplicity*—a non-unified, creatively chaotic system. All types of mind are necessary to get through each day; they compete with each other if they don't know how to work together. Knowing the right tool for the job is the art of the *shokunin*. Skillful means has "skill" on account of just the right moves, effort, turns, etc.

Optimism

*A winning mind is what you have when
you remove evaluation.*

British climbing legend Jerry Moffatt credits *With Winning in Mind,* a book by Olympic sharpshooter Lanny Bassham, for a revolution in how he thought about winning. A star on outdoor rock, Moffatt wasn't doing well in the comps in the late 1980s and 1990s. He really wanted to improve, but his mental game was weak, and he was at a loss. By chance, he found Bassham's book and went out on a limb and tried the practices. Each day he told himself he was a winner and that he was going to win. He stuck notes on the wall reminding him of this fact. He became obsessed with changing his outlook on winning. He knew it would take months, so he gave it months. It worked, and he found the top of the podium shortly thereafter.

What happened? Moffatt changed his self-image. Bassham's book doesn't so much focus on "being a winner" but on having a winner's mindset. That mindset entails believing you are the type of person that wins. "Winners are convinced they will finish first," Bassham writes. But it's more complicated than that. The winner's mindset is not an adjustment in confidence, since confidence traffics in trust. It's not quite optimism either, as that is when you think good things are going to happen. Rather, Moffat needed to change something deep about his self-image so he could focus on process *without judgement* (valuation). He reconceived his entire self as a winner to keep the non-winner thoughts from infecting his mental ecosystem. Paradoxically, despite Moffatt thinking about winning, he wasn't really thinking about winning. He was trying to change the goal and his self-image. He needed to redefine himself as the type of person that performs well. He changed the way he perceived his actions in relation to a goal. Moffat did away with instrumental movement, with leveraging his climbing against anything that wasn't climbing. Bassham writes: "And the best focus, in my view, is on a winning performance, not on finishing on top. I suggest that you goal set to have a winning performance on the day of the competition instead of goal setting to win the competition."

No stranger to success, basketball legend Michael Jordan would agree: "You have to expect things of yourself before you can do them." And yet, in the multi-part documentary *The Last Dance*, it's clear Jordan was as obsessed with winning as he was not losing. So what gives? What gives is that you *can* be motivated by just winning, but it comes at a cost, and anyone who watches the documentary can see that Jordan is actively struggling. You can see it in his eyes, his unsettled mannerisms. He doesn't seem to be content with how his career worked out, which is odd, considering he was one of the best athletes ever to have lived. Like Phelps, depression and mental fatigue were constant friends. In short, what drove them wasn't durable, nor sustainable.

The trick is changing the object of expectation, the thing you expect. You can be a 5.12/7a+ climber and tell yourself you are a winner and that you are going to win a World Cup. But the truth is, if 5.12/7a+ is your limit, you are not going to win a World Cup. I am never going to climb 5.15a/9a+. I'd like to, but it seems entirely unreasonable to direct my energy in that direction. It's equally unreasonable, at this juncture, to hope to climb something that hard as much as it is to be upset if I don't. What I need to expect from myself is a good burn on my project, to set myself up, physically and mentally, to climb well. Anything less, or more, is irrelevant. The rest takes care of itself. For all practical purposes, if you need to convince yourself that you are the type of person that performs well, you should do it. Eventually, once you have retrained your mind, you won't need to convince yourself. You will just be the person that performs well, day in and day out, and then, eventually, all that consistency will make you better, in a shorter timeframe, than if you patchwork anxiety with belief.

Success is not the podium, but it is the quality of the performance, as Bassham repeatedly observes— that is the secret sauce of winners, regardless of level. Their expectations are performance oriented, not end-goal oriented. More importantly, they don't just know this intellectually, they put the principle to work in all aspects of their athletic life, on and off the field.

There are only three flat spots on a podium, after all, and so relying on a podium to define *what a winner is* is extremely myopic, misguided and damaging.

Confidence is Overrated

Movement isn't good or bad, no different
from a tree falling in a storm.

You know what they say about guys with big trucks— they are compensating for something small. The psychology behind this is called *projection*: the big-truck guy is masking his feelings of smallness behind a projection of bigness (the truck). He is protecting his small ego from the gaze of others, who might consider him powerless, and from himself, because, in the act of possessing an image of power, he can defer working on the root cause of powerlessness.

Confidence in our minds works similarly: we need to build up our confidence to the point our sense of weakness is masked. Confidence is the belief in ability. But, as famed sports psychology theorist Ken Ravizza has noted, "confidence is overrated." On the day he became the first person to flash a 5.15a/9a+, Adam Ondra later said in an interview that: "I lacked the confidence I'd hope I'd have." Ondra said that about the hardest flash in history, a type of climbing most people think requires the highest level of confidence.

Confidence is overrated: I have found this to be true in my own climbing. When you have confidence, you set up a duality, and with every ying, there's a yang. You introduce duality, and with it a concept, and with that concept, evaluation. If you fill yourself with positive talk to build up your confidence, you are merely throwing a blanket over self-doubt. Or, at the very least, self-doubt is lurking, and you need to keep it in check. That's the mental reason for latching onto confidence in the first place—to combat the *lack* of it. Yet, the mental insecurity remains and wreaks *more* havoc on account of being suppressed, it being a fact of the human mind that everything unconscious has unpredictable, and unwarranted, influence. What you are really doing is covering self-evaluation with a short-lived psychological Band-aid: confidence.

An athlete only needs to add confidence when they are, unconsciously or not, judging themselves, as it is in this act of self-judgement that the need for positivity originates. On tennis, Gallwey writes: "Clearly, positive and negative evaluations are relative to each other. It is impossible to judge one event as positive without seeing other events as not positive or as negative. There is no way to stop just the negative side of the judgemental process. To see your strokes as they are, there is no need to attribute goodness or badness to them. The same goes for the results of your strokes. You can notice exactly how far out a ball lands without labeling it a 'bad' event. By ending judgement, you do not avoid seeing what is. Ending judgement means you neither add nor subtract from the facts before your eyes. Things appear as they are—undistorted. In this way, the mind becomes calmer." When things appear as they are, this is big mind, which is calm, which sees the turbulence of small mind rushing to make quick fixes via evaluation.

When Gallwey talks about adding or subtracting, he is talking about attachments. Higher-level attachments (attachments to success) fuel attachments to lower-level acts (calling a shot "bad"). In other words, when you walk into an art gallery and think "That's a good painting" or "That's a horrible painting," you are making this valuation based on an attachment to an idea of what you think a good painting is. But in reality, a painting just is. It is only good or bad when attachment intervenes. Dualism is an effect of small mind, or, more accurately, it is the origin of the latter. Big mind makes no distinction, no valuation. Movement is neither good nor bad.

You don't need confidence to climb hard routes— you need to train, execute and keep a clear head without distraction. These three things alone are all you need. If it is in your body's ability to do a route, pumping yourself full of positive talk isn't going to make a difference. You can convince yourself all day that you can't ride a bike, but when it comes times to ride a bike, you are going to if you know how. You don't need confidence or overconfidence. Overconfidence creates gaps in attention, making you drop your guard and botch the sequence. When you are overconfident, you don't try hard enough. Maybe your mind is at the chains while your body is at the crux. Researchers on sport psychology, Sian L. Beilock and Thomas H. Carr, note the negative effects of confidence-distraction: "This shift of focus changes what was single task performance into a dual-task situation in which controlling execution of the task at hand and worrying about the situation compete for attention."

For an athlete, body is *prima material*. We need something that looks like confidence—such as a clear, unperturbed mind—but it needs to be untethered from ego and given over to the body. When you do that, it feels like confidence, but isn't. "Confidence doesn't come from knowing that you control the outcome of a given event or moment," says Ben Bergeron, author of *Chasing Excellence*. "It comes from knowing that you control your *response* to a given event." Bergeron is right, and that is what Moffatt was working on. Ondra as well. The only thing we can control is our response, so that is what we need to focus on. Confidence should not be defined in terms of ego-belief, ability, success or even execution, but response, such that when the time arises, you will respond accordingly. *Response* is what you need to start trusting. If at this time, your ability fails you—and it will, because this is athletics and a learning process—then you don't 'fail', and your mentality won't take a hit. You haven't failed because you haven't attributed valuation to the act. You therefore won't *feel* like a failure.

Hope is Not a Strategy

At first, you might need to lie to yourself.

"The way you train reflects the way you fight. People say I'm not going to train too hard, I'm going to do this in training, but when it's time to fight I'm going to step up. There is no step up. You're just going to do what you did every day."

—*Georges St-Pierre, Canadian MMA champion*

Doubt is the most underrated psychological strategy in climbing, regardless of whether you are climbing V15/9a, 5.8/5b or WI6X. I've heard Sharma say that when he is close to sending a route, he tells himself this burn does not matter because he is going to fall. *I'll do it next time*, he tells himself. Why does he do this? It relieves the pressure, yes, but it also allows him to focus on climbing. What is attached, for Sharma, is months, maybe years of effort and sacrifice, and the weight of all that is present each time. There are hundreds of stories of climbers sending their projects when full of doubt, and if Sharma needs the hack, then it only testifies to the difficulty of climbing with the right state of mind. Hacks are not a bad strategy, they're just not ideal.

According to dependent arising, when one thing arises, so does another. When you have too much hope that something is going to happen, you need doubt to counteract it. Hope is like confidence, largely destructive. A distraction. As Canadian MMA champion Georges St-Pierre puts it succinctly, "Hope isn't a strategy." Climbers do not step up and onsight a 5.13d/8b when their redpoint is 7c+. Likewise, we rarely go from four-hanging our project to sending it the next day. Sure, it's possible, and don't discount the thought, but the truth of the matter is that St-Pierre is talking about the art of managing expectations. Hope, doubt, anxiety, confidence, overconfidence—these are manifestations of harmful expectation-management.

Successfully managing expectations is a form of awareness, of knowing your history, how you distribute effort, how your small mind works. It is one of the things that can be found in all top athletes. Better is no expectation at all, pure moment-to-moment based action. Siegrist observes: "We've all felt at times entitlement to send—that thought of 'I should have sent already!' Or 'this should be easy for me!' But over the years I've learned that this attitude is bullshit. If my goal is to be challenged and to improve, why not be open to every lesson? If it truly was 'easy,' it wouldn't be hard, would it! The moment we start assuming that everything will be easy is the moment we shut ourselves off to learning."

Learning isn't easy if not for the simple reason that you are admitting you have weaknesses. Admitting you have deep weaknesses is hard. You need to learn how to learn. Learning isn't so much a state of mind, as a state of being, that of the *shokunin*.

"Have a Think"

Climbing is not mere execution,
courtesy of distraction.

It wasn't until I started climbing with a rope that the mental aspect of climbing really came into focus. The first thing I noticed was that the rope adds duration. Duration adds complexity because the former adds time, and when time is added, the brain takes advantage and activates itself. "Climbing is psychologically demanding, because the climber has time to think. And if you have time to think, it's hard to stay in the flow," says Rudolf Tefelner, a mentor of Adam Ondra. On a rope I found myself thinking too much, or under-thinking it, or not being able to find the middle ground of being relaxed and aggressive at the same time. "The brain is the most important muscle for climbing," Wolfgang Gullich once said. But we need also to add that it is your worst enemy, too.

Tefelner is right—climbing isn't mere execution of a rehearsed routine. We are not robots executing code. We are imperfect untamed humans. Distractions introduce themselves—a bat in the crack, wind and rain; a botched clip, missing a hold and having to readjust. Mental or physical fatigue bursts our flow bubble, a situation that doesn't so much have to be avoided, as managed. Fatigue breaks down the body's ability for mindfulness, which is why we often have to *make* ourselves focus during the later sections of a route, mainly because focus will not arrive as organically as before, and so we have to summon that internal voice, "OK, just stay focused," or "Just a little bit longer." Summoning the voice isn't ideal, but it's a hack and part of being all-too-human.

In the Tokyo Olympics, the announcers were astonished by how much climbers had to think. One announcer, during the men's bouldering finals, kept saying, "...and now they need to have a think." That's right. A climber needs to analyze what they did, or think they need to do, then execute it, but while executing it, gather that feedback and carry it forward. Top athletes learn very quickly—that is the essence of the bouldering format, in particular. You only get so many minutes. Every effort counts. Most World Cups are won by very small, very crucial adjustments with only a little bit of time left on the clock, which means, even the slightest bit of hesitation or overthinking, or over trying, is the difference between the podium and sixth.

Climbing movement is a point of interface between past failures and future success, and the attentive climber manages this sieve with dexterity, whereas the inattentive climber is at the whims of what a route, or their mind, throws at them, and so just tries to hold on, literally and figuratively speaking.

Bread

*It is in moments of trying too hard
where we are most vulnerable.*

When I first saw someone make a loaf of bread, I was amazed. Despite having Sicilian and northern Italian roots, it never occurred to me that you could, just like that, make bread.

When I was growing up, bread was something we bought at the store, and it was white and lasted months, and you didn't think about it much, except not to eat too much of it at a restaurant—God forbid one should fill up on bread. But on occasion, my parents went to the Italian store in downtown Baltimore. They bought a loaf of *real* bread, and those glorious few days of fresh salami and prosciutto and capicola and mortadella with pistachio, and, of course, fresh bread, would never last long enough. Then, sure enough, days later, we were back to white bread.

Intrigued by this magic, I started to learn to bake bread. This was ten years ago. I became obsessed and learned about poolish, ciabatta, starters, kneading, slow rise. I took notes on the temperature in the kitchen. I went on Instagram and searched #sourdough. At first, I would fold the dough, but I didn't understand the *nature of dough*, and so I kept stretching it past its breaking point, which meant the gluten fibers were not strong enough to withstand what I was doing. A strong network of gluten allows the air to collect in the bread, which gives it a good rise, which makes bread airy. And so on. Then I learned I was doing it wrong, and so I started to pay attention. I knew I needed to learn. Finally, after months of paying attention, I realized I was handling the dough differently, like I knew what it wanted and was respecting that wish. I no longer had to be conscious of the pressure my hands applied to the dough. They just knew. My body just knew. It became "second nature," a telling phrase we use to denote when an artificial layer of skill has infused our bodies to such a depth that it acquires the status of a second "nature," which implies the deployment of such a skill can bypass consciousness direction and operate at a level akin to primary nature.

Now, a self-described "8b bread maker," it's clear what distinguishes an "expert" bread maker from a novice is an understanding of the materiality of dough and the willingness to keep learning. Similarly, the Chinese character for swimmer is translated as "one who knows the nature of water." As for dough, the knowledge is in how it behaves in a winter versus a summer kitchen; what an added egg does to consistency; how to form a thick crust with steam; how much longer a rise will take if your starter is only 50 percent doubled as opposed to 70 percent. And so on. The more I became aware of the dough, the more I learned why certain breads turn out the way they do. With this very same knowledge, in terms of climbing injuries, I brought myself out of years-long injury cycles simply by making it a point to listen to my body after each attempt on a hard boulder, or hard route, since the seeds of injury are here, first and foremost, in miscalibrated effort and exertion. It is in moments of trying too hard where we are most vulnerable, but it's a line climbers need to ride. I realized my injury cycle was not a result of a weakness in body, but weakness in mind. Almost every time, when I was revving my body for a hard move, I could sense the injury coming before it did, mostly on hard crimp moves. I'd overcompensate, try too hard, and push my tendons to places they were not ready to go. From that insight, I saw a pattern, and from an understanding of the pattern I made adjustments. For over 15 years, I had one or two pulley injuries a year; now I'm going on four years without a single one. The only difference I made was in paying attention, taming my recklessness and changing my habit patterns.

The body, and not just its tendons and muscles, is a reactive system akin to dough. At first, when you start paying attention, the body is complex, a stranger at times, unwieldy, mysterious, then, after years of working with it, we get complacent and it becomes simple and taken for granted, then, with age, the body becomes complex again ... but you are able to manage the complexity with simplicity.

The Body Knows

Interference is small mind made manifest.

A climb is a labyrinth of movement our bodies must navigate. If we have not taken the time to listen to our bodies, we fail them, and we will not climb to our potential. No athlete will. If you think your body needs a helicopter parent, constantly directing, insisting on this or that, micromanaging, then you are disrespecting your body's innate capabilities. The body digests, heals, keeps itself warm, fights off viruses and bacteria, all without conscious direction. Teach it to ride a bike, and it will never need to relearn, even after 50 years. It is learning and adjusting without you knowing it, all the time, in everything you do. Walk it up a mountain, and it will tell you when to slow down. The human body has been fighting off prey, surviving hard winters and forming complex human communities for tens of thousands of years, long before hyperconscious, rational thought came onto the scene. In evolutionary terms, "overthinking it" is a late arrival to the human organism, and that it arrived late in no way implies it is the most beneficial or most adaptive.

If you want to juggle, you cannot think your way to a five-ball cascade. You might be able to visualize it from watching videos, but your body will learn at its own pace. If a basketball player had to think carefully about the ball's trajectory on each bounce and how to time this with his gait and his need to change direction, in coordination with other players, little would be done. The body cannot be a chess player, considering all the scenarios before moving.

When it comes to athletics, the body needs to be able to do its thing without *interference*. When I say without interference, I am not saying no-mind. The popular notion of Zen putting a premium on "no-mind" needs to be explained carefully. It's a problem of translation—of what "mind" means to us versus what it means to Zen masters. Having no mind, as in "no brainwaves," is impossible. If you have no brainwaves, you are dead. Whether big mind or small mind, brainwaves are firing. Zen has a different perspective of mind than the scientific materialism of Western neurobiology. Zen doesn't care so much about what mind *is*, but what it *does* and what it *sees*: small mind sees what is immediate, and what is tethered to ego, personality, immediate fears, and so on. Big mind sees small mind. Mind is not just cognition, as we think of it, but an all-encompassing sense of awareness.

Zen is interested in the moments when mind becomes a hindrance (small mind) and how we can use or train the mind to relieve our suffering and delusion. Cultivating big mind is cultivating clear awareness in the body, because the clearer you can see how small mind is reacting to the body's fluctuations, the more you can manage those fluctuations. This goes for managing our emotions as much as managing ourselves on a hard climb.

Toggle Effect

*The climbing mindset is not far from that of
a trauma nurse. Look, patch up, move on.*

Similar to *the ask*, climbing might be singular as
regards the intense phenomenon that is the *toggle
effect*. It's what we love and hate about the sport,
how things go from fun in the sun to death fall in a
matter of seconds. You're cruising that multi-pitch
5.8/5b in the alpine when suddenly the sky opens
up and lightning strikes ten yards away, while you
are 25 feet from your last good cam. Or, you are
80 feet up a beautiful ice pillar when you hear that
dreaded crack deep in the ice, and you know that
one bad swing of the axe could bring the whole
thing down ... with you on it. I've been in both
these situations, a lot. The toggle effect requires
climbers to react immediately with the appropriate,
calibrated act.

When Honnold solos, he is keen to master the
toggle effect, as the stakes are so high. Which is
why, when working a route, he constantly visualizes
himself in certain positions to give his mind a dry
run of the psychology of the position—to prepare
his mind in such a way that it does not toggle into
fight or flight when he's there for the send go, but
remains in control. But, of course, toggling cannot
be avoided, just mastered. Olympic swimmer and
gold medalist Michael Phelps has said the same

thing about his mental preparation: he visualized the good and the bad, obsessively, to help prepare for the panic that the toggle often entails. It paid off. In the 2008 Olympics, during the 200-meter fly final round, Phelps' goggles filled with water. He was swimming blind. It was a worst-case scenario. But he stayed calm, knew what needed to be done, and was able to snag gold despite a setback that would have crushed most swimmers. What did he do? He kept swimming. He didn't let distraction get in the way.

Visualization is rewiring your mental ecosystem so that the shock to your neural system is either lessened, or, in the case of climbing beta, prepared to act with as little cognitive interference as possible. Visualization is a form of forward-facing memory implantation. It is cultivating a state of awareness such that when your body is pinging you with crucial information, some of it soul-crushing, it appears just as that, information, and not noise. Visualization, to be extra effective, need not be limited to imagining how things are going to go well, but visualizing how things are going to go bad. To do that, you need to look more carefully at a route, or problem, and give your body the negative sensations so it can experience in advance the pump, or the fear, or the state of mind you are going to be in.

Mistake Management

When you botch a sequence, it leaves a residue.
The what and where of that residue is often a mystery.

Too often, climbers mess up their beta and say "take," as if it were already concluded that any simple mistake will accumulate into a failure. The botched sequence is like a rock tossed into an otherwise perfect engine—now you have to drive with it rattling around, i.e., an extra pump, a frazzled mind, a sense of foreboding. However, it does help to know whether the rock will destroy the engine or just nag at you until you arrive. It also helps to know if you are *able* to drive around with a rock in the engine in the first place, and/or what it feels like to do so.

It is not happenstance that Adam Ondra, Alex Megos and Margo Hayes—some of the hardest *redpoint* climbers—are also responsible for some of the hardest onsights. Ondra onsighted 5.15a/9a+, Megos 5.14d/9a, etc. Hayes, an American, was the first woman to clip the chains on a 5.15a/9a+. The same is the case with Jimmy Webb, the best onsight boulderer of his generation and one of the strongest around.

These climbers are masters in dealing with mistakes, i.e., they can toggle with dexterity and elite attentiveness. They have the ability, mid-route or mid-sequence, to acknowledge they have just made an error and "forget" quickly. In onsighting, you rarely do any sequence perfectly, and it takes quite a bit of calculative thinking, which means you are almost always aware when you make an inefficient move. To onsight near your redpoint level, you need to master the toggle, to develop the ability to share "calculation" with "second nature" in a split second. Then, when your calculating mind tells you that you've just made a mistake, and it's over, you need to counteract that with a mental stoicism and refuse to indulge the negative entropy. Big mind doesn't get "stuck."

The skillset of onsight climbing—being able to move freely, to make bad decisions and forget about them, even to climb with conscious *inefficiency*—is also the skillset of hard redpointing. Onsighting merely magnifies aspects of hard redpointing: mistake management is top among them. The goal is to not let bad emotions appear as a result of feeling like you are going to fail. Or of feeling like a failure in the first place. If you don't have toggle release valves in life, you don't have them in climbing. Pay attention to how well you can move on, or how much you get stuck and obsess over things. If you do it in life, you do it in climbing. Release valves prevent the accumulation of negative energy in the body, the downward spirals of bad performance. In an ideal scenario, you don't need release valves because the micro-aggressions inside your body, directed against your body, never latch onto any form "I" but merely float away from the body like a vapor. Stop indulging your emotions with ownership, and they will stop owning you.

Perfection, Nope

Effortlessness is impossible, especially in climbing
Stop chasing a unicorn.

"You know when there is the feeling that everything is perfect. The day is perfect. The weather is perfect. Well, it was not that day ... I really didn't know what to expect from this attempt, so I just kept climbing and kept going."

—*Stefano Ghisolfi, Italian professional climber, on the day he got the second ascent of Change, the first 9b+ in the world.*

No send is ever perfect. Perfection is a unicorn.

Climbers will say such a send felt "perfect," that they had hit that flow state, but this only describes an internal feeling, a sensation, of a climb feeling effort-*less*, which is impossible because climbing requires a lot of effort. In reality, a lot of things are happening and effort is being masked. Effort is so perfectly calibrated it feels to the climber as though they are not trying, which is entirely different from being effortless. You can walk and not try, and it might feel effortless, but your body is expending effort.

What the claim really means is that the athlete encountered few obstacles, because the feeling of effort often pops into conscious awareness when the status quo of energy output is disrupted, or the effort they *did* put in did not generate a negative mental feedback loop. In athletics, the claim of effortlessness is a revealing sentiment because we often ascribe the flow state as the absence of something—the absence of a mistake, barrier, injury or awkwardness. Flow state is subtractive, not additive in nature. The reason for the effortless sensation might be that they actually didn't make a mistake, likely not true, or that they are dialed into mistake management, and so whatever mistakes they did make were not "red-flagged" into their somatic system (toggled). When you expect imperfection, rather than perfection, a mistake isn't a concept through which you judge a move, it's just a different kind of move, one you didn't expect.

The flow state is the exception, a sensation we seek in our training and climbing, whereas the normal is in the middle, where we cruise through the first crux, bumble through a middle part, milk the rest, then barely hold on to the chains. Preparing for the exception only creates false expectations. Preparing for the norm is the sure bet. Imperfection is the norm. On the other hand, you do need to prepare for climbing really well and not overinvesting energy in the goodness of your climbing. I've seen countless climbers fall on the easy section after the crux because they were not prepared to climb so well, and so were out of sorts when they found themselves in a place they didn't expect to be. The art of learning to manage good climbing is the same art as learning to manage bad climbing. As the poet Rudyard Kipling famously wrote: "If you can meet with triumph and disaster, And treat those two impostors just the same."

There is an internal aesthetic to climbing, in the sense that hard climbing often requires grace. Difficult climbing rewards poise, exacting effort, flirting with dance more than weightlifting, despite it feeling like the opposite. When we climb with a sense of grace, certain feelings are produced by the body, and that feeling masks effort, i.e., it can feel like effortlessness.

Climbing is easy when it feels effortless, but since that's rarely ever the case, not to mention inaccurate, it's wiser to stop chasing flow and start to develop a strategy when things are not going your way. Ironically, when you do that, flow appears more often. As Stefano Ghisolfi's example above illustrates, you can do the hardest climb of your life, when things *need* to be perfect, and yet do it when *nothing* feels perfect. Same with Ondra not feeling confident when he completed the world's hardest flash. On the day Shawn Raboutou sent *Megatron* (V17/9a), one of a handful of boulders at that grade in the world, he said, "It didn't feel like a good day. Like I didn't think I was going to do it." Colorado climber Chad Greedy, who was with Shawn that day, called the conditions "crap." It was, for most people, too hot to try hard. Still, Raboutou kept up. He didn't let the thoughts of bad conditions affect his effort.

These two examples illustrate the body's innate intelligence and how it can move and climb virtually unfazed by fickle cognition. And they illustrate the trust that top climbers have in this "lesser known" intelligence, and their rare ability to not allow negative thought patterns (small mind) to influence their body. Despite feeling suboptimal, top athletes know to keep going and not let negative thoughts influence their body's ability to do what it does best. The goal is not to deny the power of feeling, nor block emotions. The goal is to allow them to come forth with all their power, acknowledge them, get to know them, see how they move inside your mind-stream, because when you block, or ignore them, you increase their power.

Kintsugi

Execution is a state of mind.

We think that to climb at our limit, or for any top-end sports performance, we need to be flawless. We think the appearance of a mistake within a game or performance tarnishes it, and we dread a mistake because we think we need perfection to do something at our limit. But we are mistaken. Perfection is just a story we tell ourselves. We fail to realize this is athletics—perfection is a philosophical concept with no place in sports or, when you think about it, life in general.

Inspired by the philosophy of Zen, the Japanese have a centuries-old art of repairing broken things, such as pottery and vases, with a gold lacquer. The gold "glue" accentuates the break rather than hides it, and many *kintsugi* vases are more valuable *after* being broken and repaired in this manner. Why? It's an aesthetic that suits Japan's cultural mood—the

Zen idea that completion and perfection are myths. Embrace the reality of dirty, broken existence. Of a fickle body. Of a send that didn't feel right. Or no send at all. Perfection is not a physical attribute but a state of mind. See in brokenness a completion. It is a lesson in acceptance. The beauty of *kintsugi* vases is in the scars of reconstruction.

If one needs to define perfection in a performance, it should never be based on an outcome, such as a gold medal or a world record. Nearly all winners have made mistakes in their winning performance. As 16th-century swordsman and Zen master Yagyu Munenori has said, "It is an illness to think solely of winning." Rather, perfection is an attribute of execution. Execution is a readiness to confront. Being aware, unattached, clear, not trying too hard. A significant difference between an elite athlete and a midtier athlete is their approach to effort. Execution is a state of mind yoked to a body. Effort properly distributed across body and mind is skillful means. The deployment of skillful means rises in proportion to embodying big mind.

The Paradox of Trying Hard
Try hard in the right places only.

Last season, I climbed a 5.13a/7c+ mixed-gear route, though it wasn't all gear, as there were five bolts down low. I thought it would be a lot harder, but it went down rather quickly. The route was the second pitch on a beautiful granite pillar. From a hanging belay, it starts with three boulder problems over small roofs, requiring all manner of techniques—finger locks, hand jams, kneebars, pinches, good footwork. The feet are decent, but the granite is polished. The first roof is protected by a bomber finger-sized cam, then bolts for a few more roofs. Then you exit this giant chasm and find yourself in one of the most amazing positions in Western Colorado, on a giant granite spike overlooking the Crystal River Valley and our local hot springs.

The boulder problems on the route were easy enough. I didn't have to try too hard, but I had to *try*. Higher on the route, above a sketchy cam, I had to stay focused for a bad smear and slap to a polished arête, but not *really* try. I clipped the chains, and the first thought I had was *it couldn't have been 5.13a/7c+ because it felt so easy.* Yet it felt easy because my effort was calibrated. Just a few climbs over, there is a tricky 5.13b/8a I did a week before. That route is super bouldery and has a hard drive-by dyno at the second bolt, at around V8/7b. I learned that the harder I tried to do the dyno, my foot would pop, or I couldn't hold the swing. Something was miscalibrated in my effort, and I couldn't figure out what.

I realized it wasn't *trying hard* that got me, but rather I was trying hard in the wrong places. I had convinced myself I needed to try harder, and so I put the lion's share of effort into one piece of the puzzle—latching the hold. My mental energy was laser-focused on the position of my left hand in catching the edge. *If only I could catch it perfectly.* It felt obvious to do this because if I could just latch the hold, then I'd be done and take it to the chains, and I was falling because I wasn't latching the hold. Easy enough—focus on the hold, right? Wrong. It was a classic *cart before the horse* scenario because I wasn't paying enough attention to my positioning. In trying to latch the hold, I wasn't weighting my right foot, the one I was jumping off, and because I wasn't weighting it *just so,* I was dynoing too early, which meant I had too much swing. I soon realized the error was in mechanics, not effort. I had to step away mentally, become aware of what I was doing, and release myself from what I was doing. I needed to realize I was caught in a failure cycle. I was also anticipating too much. By focusing on the latch, I couldn't do the move to get there. The latch was a mental image I had become attached to, and, ironically, it clouded my ability to get there.

Some failure cycles have good reasons—such as not being strong enough, or not having enough endurance. But in this case, when I asked myself if I was strong enough, I concluded, yes, that wasn't the problem. My whole strategy was off. My ego and attachment to a way of doing things were holding me back. I only needed to release myself from the base instinct, or myopia, of trying to latch the hold. So, one night after failing, I told myself to just focus on setting up the dyno, not doing the dyno. I resolved not to latch the hold but to stand on my foot. In essence, I had to put more intelligence in my foot. I had to teach my right foot to hold the line until it was time not to. Going forward, I redefined what success looked like for this one sequence: when I stood on my foot through to the end, I had improved. And so, on my next try on the next session, I stood on my foot, made the dyno, and sent the route. It was remarkable how long it took me to step back, look carefully and figure out this simple move. Often, all we need are little breakthroughs like this. They are there all the time, in fact, but we just don't see them.

Try Too Hard, You Fail
The best way to score is not to try.

Putting in a good effort is not the same as trying hard. To try hard means effort *over and beyond* stasis energy.

An example: you are running at an easy pace, and you see someone in the distance, and you want to pass them, so you pick up the pace. That is trying. A decision was made. You "stepped on the throttle." Trying hard is relative and involves a decision. Paradoxically, we conceive of trying hard as something we need to *ask* the body to do, and yet, it's not always conscious since the body can step it up without being asked.

In athletics, you need to try hard, but the paradox is that you often fail if you try too hard. Lanny Bassham, himself an Olympic Gold Medalist who has also spent his life talking to top athletes, sums up years of research on the topic: "Trying too hard often produces negative results." Bassham continues: "Over the past 30 years, I have talked to a lot of the winners about winning. Some were National, World and Olympic Champions. I find it interesting that champions who were consciously trying to win while competing rarely do. You heard me right. They weren't TRYING to win the competitions." George Mumford, mindfulness coach to Michael Jordan and Kobe Bryant, among others, countersigns the notion: "The best way to score is to not try to score." What does not trying and trying—since you *have* to try—actually mean?

The problem: most athletes have competed in their sports the entirety of their lives, and they've never thought about what it means to try hard, or never looked at "try hard" critically. Just as we need to shift our perception of what perfection is, we need to recalibrate what trying means. Much depends, of course, on the sport.

A high jumper needs to exert max contraction over a short duration and marry these elements to technique. A 400-meter sprinter needs to introduce a different kind of effort, which is called pacing. While the last 75 meters might be a full sprint, the first 325 meters need to be a slow ooze of efficiency, or whatever their race strategy is. The longer the duration, typically the greater room for mistakes. Climbing is like running and high jumping and playing billiards in the same event. At times, you can move slow, other times you can't. Sometimes you need to pace through 25 moves of resistance. At other times you need max contraction and max output, but you can't try too hard, because if you do you run the risk of emphasizing one aspect over another. Climbing is a throttle sport, but one in which the driver is playing chess. Modern parkour-style problems are a case in point. Men's #2 in the bouldering final of the Tokyo 2020 Olympic games required a dynamic move out and left, but in order to hold the top, your right foot had to drag and catch a toe hook. The toe hook held the swing. Every competitor over-emphasized one aspect or another—either the toe hook or the dyno to the finish. Only one competitor held it, Nathaniel Coleman of Team USA, and only because he had perfect calibration in his limbs. He emphasized the right thing at the right time, with just the perfect amount of effort and non-effort. He executed, but only because his attention was dispersed properly. He didn't get too greedy with either trying to latch the hold, or just hold the toe catch. That problem alone made it possible for him to net the silver.

Trying hard means to be aware of effort in a way we are not accustomed to. Trying hard is about intensity, and because awareness is not a light switch, tonalities and range need to be better understood. There's no such thing as trying hard and not trying hard, or full mind and no mind. It's complicated—we are complicated—and there are only degrees of awareness of effort. What you can do is push your body harder at times. When you exert conscious control, you *can* burn your hand over a candle, despite the body's natural inclination to pull your hand away. It's the same with effort: the body doesn't always want to try hard. In fact, it is often not in its best interest to try hard, as that expends vital life energies and eventually leads to injury. The oryx in the African desert walks slowly, very slowly, because of the heat. It knows that moving too fast, which burns precious water and calories, isn't beneficial to its survival in such a stark landscape. At some level, our bodies know this too.

The ability to detach from too much (and inefficient) effort is also the same skill as 'detaching' from fatigue. Deploying too much strength is the same vice as deploying too little, and both are driven by the same communication failure between mind and body. While an athlete can't avoid fatigue, it is possible to see it with more clarity, and when you see it, its ability to hijack the body diminishes.

A common misperception of embodiment, or embodied living, is simply accepting what the body gives you. If you are tired, then just quit, right? If you are feeling jazzed, apply that energy. But it isn't so simple. Being fully embodied does not mean being beholden to it, but rather having the ability to discern all the signals and emotions our physicality is emitting, and then, on an intuitive level, managing the signals for a specific performance. Being yoked to the body does not mean doing everything it asks, because, like the mind, the body has its own set of intelligences, some of which will sabotage the goals you have set for it.

In 2012, Timothy Noakes, a sports scientist at the University of Cape Town, published an interesting paper on fatigue. Noakes observed that fatigue is primarily a brain-derived emotion and is specific to each athlete. Fatigue is a conservative force in the body, protecting the athlete's body from injury *before* an actual injury might occur, which means that it is an early-onset warning beacon. Noakes concludes: "The winning athlete is the one whose illusionary symptoms interfere the least with the actual performance—in much the same way that the most successful golfer is the one who does not consciously think when playing any shot." Fatigue is an abstract signal, an "illusory symptom," and like all abstractions, it is hard to tell what form it will take. In climbing, we might feel fatigue in our forearms, and then we panic. When we panic, our heart rate increases. We then sweat in our fingertips, a horrible development for climbers. Then, panicking and sweating, we make bad decisions, and so on. The key isn't the avoidance of fatigue and chasing a mystical flow state, because to be in a body is to experience fatigue, but to *see through fatigue*, to see how you are negatively reacting to it. Each body has different genetic thresholds for when it starts to send warnings. Sometimes, you have to overcome those symptoms, because those symptoms can come from elsewhere than the body in a lot of scenarios. We need to be skeptical. You are not "transcending the body," as the Olympic motto would have it. In fact, you're doing the opposite.

A well-trained athlete can exert over and beyond this natural conservation of energy without junking up the process with supra-conscious, bubble-popping awareness. A well trained body knows exactly how much energy to exert at exactly the right time, and those resistances that cue the notifications, well, they are typically coming from places inside the mind-stream. Often, though not always, those resistances are unrelated to fatigue; they originate in doubting one's ability, memories of past failures, a fear of success; generic panic. And so on. But not all bodies are well trained. Just as crucial is the reason we activate supra-awareness and ask the body to try, or likewise, why we don't want to try when it is clearly in our body's ability. Do we need to ask ourselves if our non-trying is originating in doubt? Lack of confidence? Fear? Because we don't trust our body? Are our reasons valid? Will they serve the ultimate end? Trying hard is like a Himalayan climber's dexamethasone: you only have so much, so use it wisely. Addiction will make you sloppy and dependent.

Mental Fatigue

The athlete's relationship to their body is primary.
The body will only sacrifice itself to the performance
if the relationship is healthy.

You are running a marathon and at mile 20 of 5:35 splits you want to give up. You *really* want to give up. Your body is falling apart. Your quads are shot. Your focus is lost. Everything feels heavy. Extended exertion is getting to you.

Executing is relatively easy on a boulder problem, or a route, because of the semi-limited duration. But in a cold bivi in the Himalayas, mental fatigue is so real that the desire to give up can be overwhelming. Isn't trying, then, the only and last thing you have?

Yes, you have to try—just try *differently*. When it feels like you *have to try*, it is almost always a compensatory mechanism to combat resistances deep in your somatic complex. Athletes fight entropy, the decline in energy. Often, to combat this drop in energy, you have to send mental reminders to fire muscular neurons a little extra because the current level—and what you need to succeed—is insufficient. These mental notes are the physiological structure of effort. The work to get your body to try has to be done *before* the race. That extra bit of grit and never-give-up attitude needs to come from a place in your mind that is willing and graceful about the sacrifice—the sacrifice to the performance. There's nothing the body dislikes more than being told what to do by an ungrateful person who doesn't understand it. We have things and energies inside of us that can act just like our human counterparts—they sabotage, they hide, they get resentful.

Your body needs to feel not like a whipped mule, but a loved companion. GOAT mountain runner Kilian Jornet gets asked all the time about secret training beta. One of his most common replies is: "Listen to your body." It's both that simple and that hard. Your relationship to your body, assuming you don't have the best one, cannot be healed overnight. Like any relationship, it can take years. An injured muscle, for instance, has an intelligence to it. The muscular fibers will talk to you. If it feels you are not respecting it, it will resist. An overtrained body, when pushed too far, will shut down if it doesn't get injured first.

I can say this from experience: your body will perform better when it doesn't resent what you are doing to it. This is the result of thousands of hours of mindful training, from listening carefully to my body. When you do that, your mind will change. You will become grateful for what your body does. It's humbling. That is what we are doing when we push past those pain thresholds—we are giving more, but we are asking more. To receive joy in the "more," and to continue to have that *more* (the foundation of motivation and drive, and longevity in any sporting life), the relationship with your body needs to be the best one you can have.

Body and Mind

*Disembodiment is a myth we
like to tell ourselves.*

The mind and the body are not two separate entities, but nor are they one. It's an interface, characterized by complexity and multiplicity. Like Descartes' famous dictum, Western philosophy attributed existence to the thinking mind: *cogito ergo sum*. Existence was grounded on cognition, and, for most philosophers, cognition was defined by rationality. Rationality was perceived as separate from the body, and philosophers and mathematicians from the Renaissance onwards cited the universality of science as proof the world is ordered rationally and independently of our bodies. Like the relation of math to the universe, mind existed as a thing without the body.

But our senses inform all we do, from what we think to how we think. While it can feel as though our minds oversee our bodies, a more nuanced awareness finds a manifold, complex, and creative interface. The brain, in terms of structure, is a product of biological processes, and our minds, as the sum of thoughts that happen within our brains, are twice informed by externalities: first by structure, second by a combination of the world, our bodies, and other bodies.

Rather than assume mind and body are separate most of the time, we'd do better to assume they are integrated *all of the time* and unintegrated only by virtue of appearances, that is, superficially. Dualism, after all, is a concept, and concepts are the sole product of thought. Bodies have no need of concepts to work. A mind as we know it today does not exist without a body. The developing and relatively recent field of embodied cognition has made its fundamental assumptions public—disembodiment is a myth: the mind and body are integral. And all the talk from artificial intelligence circles about downloading our brains onto cloud-based servers remains stuck in a simple problem: we still don't know how to make a computer conscious, which is one of the primary ways we define consciousness. In short, we can't imagine a brain without a body because such a scenario is effectively impossible, because brains are biological. If we ever do achieve intelligent, conscious AI, it will not be a brain. The point—when we change our deep-seated habits of thinking that our body takes orders from a master server, such as our brain, we really start to open up new manners of being. One of those new manners, which will be renovated, is sport.

Calibration

Trying too hard and not trying enough
have the same effect.

We all know that person at the gym trying really hard to crimp their way up their first V8. They are laser-focused on crimping just right. You can see it in their beady eyes, the way they ritualize grabbing the crimp and locking it in … but, alas, their footwork is wobbly and unweighted. Their focus on the hold has blocked out focus on their feet, and, in the end, it is bad footwork to blame when they hit the mats.

The irony is that climbing hard doesn't reward this type of effort. Sure, you will see Sharma and Webb and Ondra scream now and again, but watch 100 videos of 5.15a/9a+ and V15/9a climbing, and you will notice the vast majority, I'd wager 95 percent, show the climber floating to the top, with little more than a grimace. Ethan Pringle on *Jumbo Love* is a case in point, a slow, alert stroll to the chains, as is anything by Seb Bouin, Margo Hayes, Brooke Raboutou, Lynn Hill or Stefano Ghisolfi. Perfection—not what you add to a climb, but what you take away.

Climbers need to learn how to erase wasted effort: both trying too hard and not trying hard enough. Acute awareness makes this calibration possible, while perfected embodiment follows through. Watch World Cups—the climbers are patient, stoic, most unmoved. "Calibrate" is a word we use to describe the process of adjusting a device for a specific function, or range of variables, the latter serving as the reference point. In terms of climbing, your beta is the reference point, the baseline through which you calibrate movement. Within movement is effort. Calibration is attuning oneself for the required deviations in a route or boulder problem, which might include, in some scenarios, being sloppy for a few moves, or being stiff, if that's what the job requires. Calibration isn't done once, say, before you set up a route. Rather, it is an ongoing task, completed instinctively all through a route (the toggle). Our bodies do it naturally every second, like a refresh button loading the current status of vitality. Sometimes we have to calibrate consciously, such as forcing ourselves to have an extra rest after getting unusually pumped. The variables that determine a climber's calibration are only known to the climber and can never be fully revealed. In general, it is advised to expend as little effort as possible, just up to that point where it's barely enough. Calibration and efficiency are connected at the hip on this front, especially for the endurance aspects of climbing. A top marathon runner might think in terms of running economy, a mix of efficient stride, exertion, oxygen intake and a host of other factors, which, once mastered, helps the athlete calibrate the required effort. Better running economy means less conscious management of effort.

Perfection is perfect calibration, and for perfect calibration, the work needs to be done instinctively and outside the parameters of calculative thinking. Of course, you need to have a think about your climbing, and think hard, but it is just one tool we have, and, in general, supra-cognitive processes (small mind) have no place in actual performance.

Cat on a String

To be in our limbs, and yet to be free,
is not a contradiction.

"The mind is not to be treated like a cat tied to a string. The mind must be left to itself, utterly free to move about according to its own nature. Not to localize it is the end of spiritual training. When it is nowhere it is everywhere."

—*Takuan Soho, 16th-century Zen master, poet, painter*

The Zen philosophies of no-mind seem paradoxical—and often absurd. On the one hand, we are to empty the mind, remove distraction, and focus on the present, whether we are cooking rice, sweeping the leaves, chopping wood, or climbing 8b+. It makes sense. Remove small mind and all its petty problems. On the other hand, we have quotes like the one above, telling us that: "The mind must be left to itself, utterly free to move about according to its own nature." How does the mind move about "according to its own nature?"

Big mind is our essential nature. Small mind is equally mind, but it is a wave in the ocean, not the ocean itself. Tefelner, a performance psychology coach, says of Ondra, "He is just not afraid to fall. He is just and only focused on his arms, legs and climbing. He doesn't even realize he is high up, so every move can be absolute." Absolute is an odd way to describe climbing movement, but when you think about it, Tefelner means simply that Ondra's movements are not diminished, not blocked, which is the first definition of absolute: "not diminished." Perfection—the art of taking away. Or, we can add, *returning to something original*. That Zen thinkers use big mind and original mind interchangeably isn't a coincidence. Original means first nature.

Ondra is not the world's best climber in spite of this skill, he is the world's best *because of* this skill. Focus, then, isn't necessarily an attribute of Ondra's mind, it is of a mind-body interface, defined by full embodiment (arms, legs, etc). In movement science, it's called *proprioception*: the ability for you to have awareness of your body's location and position in space. It is acknowledging the intelligence outside of the traditional seat of your mind —your head—and creating an awareness pipeline from your limbs to central command: your frontal lobe. It is coming to terms with our octopus nature, that of an animal with brains in its limbs. While we don't have brains in our limbs, there are hundreds of types of intelligence the body gives us during any one moment. For climbers, the slip of a fingertip on a hold is an intelligent signal. We need to react to it. A shake in our leg. We need to react. Forearms that don't recover. React. Few sports demand such intense proprioception as climbing.

While it might seem these two directives—to be in our limbs, and yet to be free—are contradictory, they aren't. It is the same mechanism as with yoga, and the freedom of being yoked. They are saying the same thing. Mental entrapment is the unmoored mind, at the whims of externality. To achieve complex movement, which Ondra says he loves most about hard climbing, your mind—not the same as calculative consciousness—needs to be able to "travel" across your body and inhabit whatever area is needed most (pure embodiment). That is what Takuan means when he says mind is everywhere but nowhere (big mind). Calibrated execution occurs when a spotlight can scan an area at will, in real time, with no blockages. Here, mind means attention, in a sense. Blockages can be attachments, stubbornness, fatigue, and so on, preventing the spotlight from moving. Blockages only live in small mind. Blockages can also manifest in the pipeline of information coming from our limbs to our mind. It is not just that mind is going to our limbs, but rather, that is a convenient metaphor. All parts of our bodies share in mind, since there is no part of physicality that is not manifested in thought, in one way or another. Mind is inclusive of everything, but it doesn't not mean what we see is doctored. It is possible to have direct experience of our bodies, just as it is possible to have direct experience of nature, what Zen would call *is*ness or *such*ness.

Unfortunately, our brain cannot focus properly on two things at once, and so when you overemphasize grabbing a certain hold, you are blocking out awareness of other body parts. The solution isn't so much to have awareness *nowhere*, though that does work in some situations, but to inhabit the body's geography only where needed, what management and production theorists call JIT—just in time. JIT means not producing energy, or motion, in surplus, in deficit, nor before or after that energy is needed. JIT is energy produced in real time, with intelligent calibration, with optimized embodiment.

Bruce Lee was adamant that having no style in martial arts was essential. Why? Because in a street fight, there are no rules, and style constricts one's movements because it creates predictable patterns that are vulnerabilities in a fight: the fighter can't react, or is trained to a narrow focus. Lee is talking about blockages, and the defining feature of his martial arts was removing them. Style is a block. Lee writes: "Be like water making its way through cracks. Do not be assertive, but adjust to the object, and you shall find a way around or through it. If nothing within you stays rigid, outward things will disclose themselves. Empty your mind, be formless. Shapeless, like water. If you put water into a cup, it becomes the cup. You put water into a bottle and it becomes the bottle. You put it in a teapot, it becomes the teapot. Now, water can flow, or it can crash. Be water, my friend." Translated to the athletic body—allow mind, which is shapeless, to flow into any shape (arm, leg, finger, palm). Practice walking and putting your mind into senses—what you hear, what you smell. The sensate focus you learn in this exercise can be directly translated to putting mind into your body when climbing.

Samurai and Filling the Body with Mind

Ice is a language. Slopers, crimps, ice tools, all have a language. Experience is the only teacher.

D.T. Suzuki, one of the foremost Zen thinkers of the 20th century, wrote at length on Zen philosophy and the samurai. Zen had a huge influence on the warriors. Zen taught samurai a practical way to confront death by helping rid them of ego-thinking, but it also gave them a *way* to fight.

Master samurai aspired to the point of mindless automatism, where the body knew what to do, how to react, without conscious interference or calculation. More specifically, the samurai's arms knew just how to move in perfect lockstep with an enemy's sword, and their feet knew how to position themselves naturally. It took years and years of training the mind and body complex, years to dampen interference (nerves, fear, hesitation, anxiety, trepidation), and no amount of technical skill and know-how could compensate for an untrained mind. This ability was highly prized and the mark of a samurai master. Takuan's letter: "When the ultimate perfection is attained, the body and limbs perform by themselves what is assigned to them to do with no interference from the mind."

Ultimate perfection is not unlike Ondra's absolute. But *who* is assigning *what* to the body and limbs? The question has a few answers. First, the *outside*—in this case, the enemy—is making the assignment. Lee wrote about adjusting "to the object," namely, another fighter, and the same applies here. If the enemy strikes hard down the middle, that is the first part of the assignment. For climbers, that is a hold, or, more generally, a route: moving on certain holds, allowing our body to cater to the hold, and not trying to force the movement up the stone. The stone is a language. Ice is a language. Slopers, crimps, ice tools, all are a medium, and every medium has a language. When you climb ice, you need to listen; hearing is more important than seeing on a lot of occasions. A good stick has a sweet thud to it, and the tool vibrates just enough, sending back signals to your hand. When you climb on subpar rock or flakes, you knock. You listen for hollowness. The language of the rock climber's medium (the holds) has directionality, speed, thresholds, potential for connectivity among these factors; a hold will tell you if you can camp out on it and get a rest, or if it's a bump. The shape and angle of a sidepull will dictate if you need to backstep or highstep; a left-angling foot smear can only be used in a precise way. Mediums come with ideal behaviors we need to develop.

The features of stone have embedded within them a movement, and climbing movement is a meeting of two materialities: biology and geography. It takes years to decode the language, and then, after more years, we can do it without even having to think about it. It becomes second nature. As a stone sculptor, one of the first things I pay attention to when working with new stone is how it chips. Light strokes or powerful strokes. Marble requires the latter, alabaster the former. How big are the shards? Does the stone bruise? You have to pay attention to the angle of your chisel, the drawback of your manner, the existing fracture lines in the block, when to switch tools, etc. It's another language of stone. Climbing is analogous.

Each crag has a meta-language within the language, a nuance of the form of the rock and the type of rock. Sandstone is best held a certain way, granite another. Experience is the only teacher. We need to see not only the required body position, but the transitions into and out of positions. This is an abstract way of seeing, a synthesis of different levels of information becoming one. It is also an embodied way of seeing, an extension of physicality into space, a form of somatic intelligence. Listening is a meta-level approach, not a tactic. Attachments in their various forms prevent acute listening and create blockages. Takuan again: "Not to localize it [mind] is the end of spiritual training." Note that Takuan says spiritual training, not physical training. I've taken the same approach—in order to find our potential in physical training, we need to take a holistic approach.

When climbing, the body and limbs get an assignment from a fluid body-mind relation in real time. In truth, it is important not to say it is body or mind, but rather a joint operation, or, more precisely, a body and mind in an imperfect union, a union whose qualities are presence, vigilance, emptiness, whose malfunction is distraction, second guessing, wishful thinking, anxiety, etc. The waves of small mind crashing within big mind. Because we are in a time-stream, whether red-pointing or onsighting, we need near-instantaneous reaction. Why? Reaction time adds duration. Duration often, but not always, induces consciousness. Consciousness breeds complexity. Complexity is the enemy of efficient execution because complexity introduces more opportunity for error, not to mention the fact that increased cognition can actually inhibit muscles from firing at their full potential (cerebral inhibition). Remember, if you are trying to think during an activity that requires muscular exertion, your muscular output diminishes by 13 percent, a loss that will lead to certain failure when you are trying too hard, for the very reason that if something is at your limit, you need 100 percent. Because humans can perform fine motor skills, we have developed more gray matter in our spinal cords, which can inhibit our ability to fire all our muscle fibers at once. Such is not the case for apes. This is the structure at a high level—at the "local" level, we simply botch our sequence, forget something and take the whip.

Takuan continues: "The thing is not to try to localize the mind anywhere but to let it fill up the whole body, let it flow throughout the totality of your being. When this happens you use the hands when they are needed, you use the legs or the eyes when they are needed, and no time or no extra energy will be wasted." I.e., you climb a little more like Ondra.

Car Racing

Freedom is only found when yoked to your body.

Letting go is hard. Having no style, trusting the body to execute, or unyoking the mind from attachment: all these are forms of letting go and removing blockages. It's difficult stuff. Not only letting go, but a certain surrender to the materiality of our medium, which must accompany a vigilant reactive system that does anything but surrender. Climbing can be as yogic as yoga if you let it. Zen master Thich Nhat Hanh has said repeatedly there is nothing closer to your mind than your body. Anytime you work with the latter, you are working with the former.

Body and mind only find freedom, spontaneity, and, more importantly, integration when yoked together. It is a mistake to think detachment in the meditative and yogic traditions means detachment from body. That is where the Olympic imperative to "transcend the body" gets its deep (and romantic) inspiration from: religion. But we've had it wrong all these years. Yoking body to mind means full embodiment. More precisely, detachment means finding the place (big mind) where you are unmoved from the ups and downs of the small mind. Small mind never goes away as long as you are in the body. Rather, what happens is small mind comes into focus, is rendered clear. In spiritual terms, the meditative traditions call this union of *samadhi*—the union of person and tool. In the West, we call this enlightenment, but it is best described as simply being awake.

But there are risks: let go when you are not ready, and you run a risk. Chogyam Trungpa, a Tibetan Buddhist master, observed:

"For example, a professional driver in an auto race can drive at two hundred miles an hour on the racetrack because of his training. He knows the limits of the engine and the steering and the tires; he knows the weight of the car, the road conditions, and the weather conditions. So he can drive fast without it becoming suicidal. Instead, it becomes a dance. But if you play with letting go before you have established a proper connection with discipline, then it is quite dangerous. If you are learning to ski and you try to let go and relax at an early level of your athletic training, you might easily fracture a bone. So if you mimic letting go, you may run into trouble."

It is, of course, generally not physically dangerous for a boulderer or sport climber to practice letting go, but it definitely is for a soloist or bold trad or ice climber. Still, the setbacks can feel real in terms of not understanding how to solve the boulder problem or sequence and then undervaluing the act because of the frustration generated from this lack of understanding. If you build too quickly, you build with instability. If you violate your competence—a pact between you and your body—you put yourself in situations you should *not* be in. You can set yourself back months, years even. This happened to me once when ice climbing. I got into a position with bad screws, and rotten ice and mud-rock above me, and I couldn't downclimb or lower. I had to go up. It was a do-or-die situation, and so I topped out, rather shaken. Afterwards my nerves were unstable for months. I stopped ice climbing for that season, cold turkey. When you push it too far, at best it manifests in hesitation, at worst fatal error. The nerves cannot be rationally controlled because the affliction causing them to arise didn't begin rationally. The affliction is based on an inability to integrate one experience (the traumatic one) into others. So, the trauma is on the one hand attached to this prior moment, but because you are putting your body in analogous situations, it is awakened.

In terms of performance, you are simply setting yourself back. Honnold made a point of noting this fact in his talk with Armita Golkar, a sports psychologist who has studied risk: "If you exceed your comfort zone by too big of a degree, you basically have a traumatizing experience, and that kind of sets you back in terms of overall growth." When you violate the pact you have with your body, the body resists with an intelligence far superior to the one (your small mind) that gave it trauma in the first place. Nerves and a generic feeling of being "off," or unmotivated, will always grow at the site of trauma. To reverse the trauma, according to climber and mental coach Hazel Findlay, it is advised to bring back the stressors carefully and monitor how you are doing. Tread carefully. Don't overdo it. No one comes to climbing with a clean slate, and it's more often the case that people bring prior, subconscious fears to climbing, which are then exacerbated in climbing situations. Additionally, as Hazel notes, we are never finished with this type of mental training. It takes constant, diligent, intentional work.

Zone

It is impossible to overcome yourself.

David Meggyesy, a former professional football player, writes: "The zone is the essence of the athletic experience, and those moments of going beyond yourself are the underlying allure of sport."

Meggyesy's observation is a common trope in sport psychology, namely that most top athletes chase the zone, or that we all should do this. Zone is the essence of sport. Going beyond yourself is the reason we do sport. Climbers speak like this. Dean Potter, the legendary Yosemite soloist and speed climber, spoke like this, as if the zone were a mindless zombie state of pure unthinking. A single focus on task. Unwavering. Imperturbable. Mystical. Aside from being impossible, it's a myth, and I couldn't disagree more. The zone is part of sport, yes, but the "underlying allure?" No.

Sports philosophy has long been allied to the notion of transcendence, that Olympic moment of breaking barriers, going out of the body and achieving the impossible. The zone theory—'going beyond oneself'—is but a modern expression of this and finds itself implicated in the pseudo-spirituality of sport transcendence, zone philosophy included. This is unfortunate because all the best moments of sport, of being an athlete, result from being in a body to the fullest, not being detached from it. This isn't to say that some variations of zone theory don't speak of embodiment. They do. Rather, what concerns me is how this technical theory of athletic experience flows down to the general population, where it becomes warped.

Being in a body fully is no different than the feeling of being outside of one. It's not a paradox.

The zone is held up as the high watermark of athletic experience, but in reality, Honnold's observation is more accurate: "Constant improvement is the most satisfying." Sure, the ecstasy of the zone transcendence is great, but if 99 percent of the time we are aiming for the 1 percent experience, we have failed to appreciate the core of the athletic life. We have devalued the starting point. The starting point of any athlete is not to go beyond oneself, but to inhabit oneself, and, yes, that means not going *beyond* small mind—because small mind is not an experience per se, more of a vantage point—but knowing the latter with great intimacy. You can't escape small mind, only free yourself from its clutches.

The athletic life is much more than about peak experience. In fact, "peak performance" philosophy often fails to mention that peak experience is not the same as peak performance. Countless examples in the world of climbing testify to this fact, that of climbing well but feeling off center, and the examples of the latter far outnumber the cases of feeling great and climbing great. Great failures are nearly always more memorable, and impactful, than easy sends. Peak experience is about execution and can just as easily occur on your mid-level warm-ups instead of the send. Remember, perfection isn't perfect. A peak performance contains more flaws than one can count. I've sent some of my hardest boulders while in a state of profound doubt, bad conditions and on high-gravity days, like Ghisolfi. Yoke a redefined peak performance to a redefined peak experience and see what happens. Redefined, peak experience will always encompass peak performance, because a quality experience in athletics is a quality performance. Performance is not end-goal calibrated, but is now calibrated to the reference point of composure, execution and focus, among others. All these things do cater to the end-goal of doing a route, it is just that we are not motivated by the outcome, and it isn't really a goal in the traditional sense, but rather an acknowledgment of the *game of the top*. The irony of the zone is that the more you chase it, the less likely you are to find it. This is on account of the supra-consciousness that comes with chasing anything, which, in the end, prevents the very same focus you are trying to embody.

Flow is a Distraction

Don't let one process ruin the next one.
Fighting negative entropy is a supreme athletic skill.

Flow is a close cousin of the zone. Like getting into the zone, you might be able to get into the flow, but it should never be a goal. Mihaly Csikszentmihalyi, the researcher responsible for evangelizing flow theory, defined it as "a state in which people are so involved in an activity that nothing else seems to matter; the experience is so enjoyable that people will continue to do it even at great cost, for the sheer sake of doing it." Flow is about happiness and much more than athletics. It's about living creatively, with intent, and being challenged appropriately. Doing something for the sake of doing it is indeed the point—*autotelic*, as the Greeks would say—but the problem is that people end up chasing the state rather than the act. Csikszentmihalyi is not at fault, just the way his ideas were received.

As for athletics, flow is an elite experience and does not reflect the reasons we do sport. Just as many people in church might not attend because they seek mystical union with God, most athletes do not toil and train five to six hours a day, year over year, to find flow. We won't turn it down, of course. The reasons for a life dedicated to athletics are too complex, and those days training in your basement can be the most sustaining. For years, while I was getting my PhD in the Philosophy of Religion in Syracuse, NY, my training partner Buzz and I climbed in my attic every week of the year, often twice a week when the weather was shit, which was all the time. The attic was gross, 80 years of dust coated on everything, either frigid or skinripping hot, but those sessions were the highlight of my years there, hands down. Just climbing, laughing, talking shit and trying hard. If flow experiences are the best, then one would suspect those experiences are the most memorable. But they aren't. On the Tim Ferriss podcast, Olympic gold medalist Grant Hackett notes: "Then I raced the 1,500-meter freestyle and I actually had to deal with a partially collapsed lung on my left side because it was blocked with mucus for so long that that race, I probably pushed myself through more pain than I've ever had … so that race to win that gold medal was the most painful moment that I've ever had in my career. But probably the most rewarding at the same time." No flow, no zone, not enjoyable, yet the most rewarding.

Nalle Hukkataival, author of the world's first V17/9a, would reiterate exactly Grant Hackett's observation on what is most memorable in sport: "Not succeeding is an important part of the process. The most memorable things in life are not the ones that came effortlessly—no matter how impressive—but the ones you struggled with and overcame in the end."

Flow does exist, but it's not the most rewarding or enjoyable of athletic experience. Flow is the special-effects light show inside our bodies. I've experienced it a lot, but I've found it to be a distraction and another form of attachment. We seek it. We think we should. In its absence, we feel short-changed. We chase the unicorn of performance. Worse, we think we need to be in a flow state to do our best. Csikszentmihalyi says flow is "so enjoyable," but enjoying something, as Hackett's example illustrates, in no way translates to a deep satisfaction with that thing.

Undoubtedly, enjoying something is essential to motivation, but if I had to choose between enjoyment and deep satisfaction, I'd choose the latter. Satisfaction is realism. Life contains mistakes, and nearly all performances are not fully enjoyable, and so, like perfection and the zone, flow needs to be redefined in terms of how we flow *despite mistakes*, not in the absence of them. The one who flows the best, perhaps, does not flow through perfectly executed moves but rather flows from a botched sequence to a perfectly executed one, then back to botch: this is the marriage of peak experience and peak performance, to the point where the two are indistinguishable. This is the discipline of *the toggle*.

This is an expression of free mind, big mind coming into form, and not getting blocked by small mind. The climber with flow does not allow a mistake to create a block (Takuan's blockages). The mind does not become attached to a perceived failure but rather resets itself, again and again, mind moving freely across the body during performance and allowing the body's intelligence to inform decision making, a complex loop. For example, you mess up the crux sequence and suddenly panic, and have to figure it all out in a millisecond. Your world is crumbling. In management theory, it's called the *bottleneck*: when one process fails, the entire system stalls. In team building, it will get referred to as the *weakest link* phenomenon. In climbing, you don't want mistakes to become bottlenecks, just part of the execution process. If you manage expectations properly, you will manage anticipation. If you manage anticipation, you manage nerves. The trick isn't to try to control but to master your reaction, to adjust or remove expectation.

It might sound easy, but accepting failure, and working with failure, even embracing it, is one of the most productive, yet counterintuitive, things you can do in life, and in climbing. You can only do it successfully in the latter if you do it in the former. If you are an insecure person, it will show in your climbing. If you are an idealist, you will overestimate yourself and underestimate the climb. If you are a controlling person, you will avoid moments, and moves, when you don't feel one hundred percent in control.

The IKEA Effect

Distinguish between dumb effort and right effort.

In the 1950s, instant cake mixes were brought to market, requiring only the addition of water. Quickly, however, there was resistance from homemakers, which, the researchers concluded, was attributable to the fact that the mixes made 'cooking *too* easy.'

Initially stumped, manufacturers caught on and then in future mixes required the addition of an egg, which was unnecessary for the product, yet essential for the consumer's psychology. The solution made it more laborious and inefficient for consumers, but it added value because it added effort. In 2011, researchers called the phenomenon the "IKEA effect." The effect was described as: "labor alone can be sufficient to induce greater liking for the fruits of one's labor: even constructing a standardized bureau, an arduous, solitary task, can lead people to overvalue their (often poorly constructed) creations." In other words, we overvalue things the more effort we put into them, which is another way of saying that chasing the feeling of effortlessness, aka flow or the zone, is in fact to chase those moments we value the least because they are unpredictable. Effort, going above and beyond stasis, generates value. While everything in life needs effort, we need to distinguish between dumb effort and right effort. Right effort is the same as right practice. Dumb effort is misaligned to the task, despite intensity and good intention. Right effort could be less intense, or more intense, but it's more effective. Dumb effort is overpowering, or ego-driven motivation. Dumb effort is a manifestation of ignorance.

Control Freaks

Stiffness is mind made visible.
Hesitation is mind made visible.

We all know control freaks. They want to micromanage everything, from how you drive to what kind of gear you bring for a climb. They cut their toothbrushes in half to save weight on alpine climbs. They say "take" when things don't feel perfect on a sport route. They obsess over getting things just how they want them. When expectation does not match reality, bad feelings shut down their performance: a blockage manifests.

Control freaks are the worst type of parents, friends and climbing partners, but they often make pretty good climbers, at least up to a certain point. Climbing rewards control, precision and hyper-awareness, but only so far. From what I've observed after being in the game for decades, control freaks quickly plateau in their ability more often than others because the phenomenon of being *out of control*—of letting go, of confronting the X-factor and learning from it— is too uncomfortable. They are not prepared for the toggle it requires. They feel defeated when they have to really go for something. When they do, their body stiffens, lacking the necessary fluidity to do hard moves. Of course, you have to be in control, but you need to make sure non-control is driving control. Non-control is big mind. Small mind wants always to grasp, to have things the way it wants it. It is not that a climber needs to be in control, nor be out of control. You need to have the right mind for the occasion. In truth, control and non-control are simply concepts at the extremes of states of mind. Mind should be able to take any form it wants.

Climbing can aid in the struggle, but, in the end, you have to extinguish control in life to extinguish it at the crag. The only thing we can control is our reaction. Control freaks have an overdeveloped superego that needs to helicopter parent the body's natural intuition, turning what should look like a seven-year-old on a playset—flowing, loose, fun—into a whipped stable horse.

In climbing, the body will *not* naturally be stiff and controlled. That is not its natural state, just as small mind is not our original nature. When our body is stiff and controlled, it is being hacked by a hyper-conscious mind. Stiffness is small mind made visible. Hesitation is small mind made visible. Flowing limbs, calibrated effort, no real-time evaluations of acts, toggling in and out of perfected effort—that is big mind made manifest in the body, or, more precisely, that is pure relationality of the mind and body.

As Timothy Gallwey makes painfully clear, control issues often come down to trust. Self 1, which is the mind, is lashing out at Self 2, the body, for messing up, for not doing what it asked, or for making the "I" feel ashamed or inadequate. So, to take control and reassert itself as the locus of power, Self 1 micro-manages the body. The rationale for wanting to control is the same one that seeks power. Power is sought for many reasons, but it is largely—in life *and* climbing—a symptom of insecurity. Someone who does not feel powerful on the inside projects it onto their bodies, onto others and external things. Referencing French theorist Michel Foucault, the athlete's mind controls to the point that it accumulates knowledge: knowledge of the body. But since our panopticon mind constructs itself on the surveillance model, we are self-sabotaging and creating prisoners of ourselves with overactive self-criticism, fueled by judgement. Small mind advances its own interests, which is more control. When we survey ourselves, we are, in essence, normalizing mistreatment. This creates rebellion, pent-up hostility, and later, docility and a broken spirit. In climbing, it manifests as stiffness and an ignorance as to why the body just did what it did. Let go of power to regain it. Kilian Jornet says it best when he states: "Sport is above all accepting the uncertain." The uncertain is the X-factor, and all athletics has a version of it.

Pressure into Opportunity

Pressure needs to be managed before the whistle.

The *X-factor* is a moment, an "event" as so many French and German philosophers called it—an unforeseen. Elite climbers know how to deal with the X-factor not because climbing is more predictable for them, but because they have trained their bodies *not* to react in a certain way. Top climbers are defined in what they *don't do* as much in what they do.

Imagine a beginner is on their first 5.9/5c gear lead. They are cruxing out and fumbling their gear and proceed to drop the rack of stoppers. Their legs start to shake. Their hands are sweaty. They are getting pumped, fast. Their mind is racing, presenting so many options, yet all options are fuzzy and fickle.

They trust no single thought. Focus is impossible. They fall onto the ledge below and break their hip. You could say the accident started the moment they tried a 5.9/5c because they were clearly not prepared ... but this is climbing, after all, and that's the game. Plus, they were capable of climbing 5.11d/7a, just not on gear. Risk is a constant presence, and you cannot make climbing completely safe. *The ask* is an ever-present threat.

Put a pro in the same situation, but make the climb their limit, say an 5.14a/8b+ gear route, and the reaction will be completely different, despite being at their limit. They will be composed. No shaking legs. No panic. They see the panic coming, they knew it was coming, but they have the discipline of mind to stay focused since doing moves is the only safe exit.

Managing panic, stress and fear is one of the most opaque arts for any athlete, mainly because our limbic system primarily works below our conscious radar *before* it reaches consciousness. This means that most of the time, when fear or panic enters consciousness, our bodies have *already* prepped for war, quite literally. The instinctual reaction is animalistic and serves an evolutionary purpose to confront enemies: sweaty palms, hyper alertness, intensely reactive, increased heart rate, and so on. Our pupils dilate, our blood flow increases, our airways expand and our blood sugar increases to provide immediate energy. Quite literally, the body is preparing to fight. The chemical dump is the result of adrenaline and cortisol.

The problem for climbers is twofold. First, in most cases these responses are not helpful. Second, when we are in these states, the logical processes in our brains are disabled. Perhaps for alpinists or mountaineers, who have to summon the survival reserves in epics, they can serve a purpose, but on a hard sport route or hard boulder, which are closer to artful performances, the body going into a war dance is a liability rather than a net benefit. Not too long ago, neuroscientists studied Honnold's brain, concluding that his amygdala doesn't fire like the rest of ours. In short, Honnold does not suffer an "amygdala hijack," which is what 99.9 percent of climbers experience in varying degrees, in varying occasions. Sometimes we know it is coming and we can talk ourselves out of it at a good rest. Sometimes we don't know it until we take a whip and find ourselves abnormally out of breath, the adrenaline already having done its damage on the type of focus we really need. But adrenaline focus is typically not the climber's cocktail. We need dispersed, relaxed focus. We need a feather rather than a hammer, and adrenaline gives us the hammer whereas mindful effort gives us the feather.

While you can sometimes micro-manage the arrival of stress mid-route, you cannot macro-manage at that moment. Managing stress requires constant practice and a deeper awareness than simply artificial self-talk. Joseph LeDoux, one of the researchers who studied Honnold, says, "His brain is probably predisposed to be less reactive to threats that other people would be naturally responsive to, simply because of the choices he's made." While Honnold was born with a particular ability to mitigate fear, the things he has done, as LeDoux notes, have made it possible for him to react less. Honnold visualizes on a level most are unable to. He imagines the positions he will be in. He spends countless hours expanding, and causing to recede, the situations that would produce a stress reaction. Alex has done the work and rewired his brain over seasons. Moreover, he knows he is doing it. He is constantly learning. He is trying to take the question mark out of what he will encounter.

Perfection in climbing is not defined by getting to the top but by how you react. Bassham acutely observes: "Your success is determined by how well you can control what is in front of you, not by worrying about outcome." If there is any modicum of control in climbing, it is not in the outcome but what is in front of you. You can't control the holds you were given. You must surrender yet proactively react. An athlete who doesn't buckle under pressure has handled the pressure long before the whistle.

Composure

You have to allow your reservoir to fill.

A seasoned climber has a deep reservoir, but that reservoir did not get filled overnight. Mental composure is a mix of physical ability, experience, trust in body and mind, familiarity with nerves, and so on. There exists, at any moment, space for analysis if needed. They are free. Minds untethered, free to roam. Ondra talks about the "language of chalk," which means he has the ability—aka mental bandwidth—to analyze the nuances of chalk on certain holds while onsighting at his physical limit. There is no better example of the toggle than that of Ondra cruxing out, for the first time, on a 5.15a/9a+ onsight all the while noting, somewhere deep inside his mind, that the next hold is best for his right hand because he sees a chalked thumb placement on the left part of the hold.

More importantly, such athletes have *allowed* the reservoir to fill—each prior experience is reflective, whether conscious or not. Each experience of fear taught them something about how they react and don't react. Each climb allowed the climber to evolve. They learn. It's a practice. While climbing with attention may be a matter of subtracting, adding, or intelligent accumulation, it is a key piece in the war chest of climber wisdom. I heard Michael Phelps rattle off in an interview his multiple split times during five races, to the accuracy of a hundredths of a second, more than ten years after the race. How? He had studied, analyzed, and digested that race, carrying it into the future as an active memory, not a passive one. For Phelps, it wasn't a matter of remembering the splits, it was a matter of forgetting them, of not obsessing over them. Likewise, route climbers need to have in their working memory fifty moves or more, each move involving multiple sub-moves. Climbers have a lot to memorize, and we need to be able to keep that information below the surface and both call it up mid route, should we need it. Exactly what to carry forward is the challenge, but it is less so the more you are aware *during* the performance.

Wu Wei

The closer you look, the sharper the knife.

"The highest virtue is to act without a sense of self."
Lao Tzu, verse 38, Tao Te Ching

In Taoism, *wu wei* is the name for non-doing, non-action or actionless action. In Taoism, the concept brings notions of mystical energies in the universe to which we need to align ourselves, much like *ki* energy in aikido or *chi* in Chinese healing arts. It is very similar to what I have been describing here: non-trying doesn't mean doing nothing. Nor does it mean you are expending no effort. Nor does it mean you are not discerning. Rather, right effort is required. Non-trying means not activating the "trying area" of our minds and not calling up the calculative or overly analytic aspects because they bring valuation to our acts; non-effort is indeed the holy grail of performance, a form of "ultimate perfection" and absolute movement. Non-trying is relinquishing control, the controlling mind.

Great freedom is found in taking things as they come, allowing the moment in all its simple complexity to arrive unadorned of our expectations, fear, projections and desires ... through ridding ourselves of attachments and resistances. We accomplish this by looking closely at ourselves, taking inspiration from the meditative arts, and cultivating big mind. We need to be savage, however. We need to be honest with what we find inside ourselves. Only by looking inside to what we bring with us to climbing can we discover how it affects our climbing, for better or worse. A strange phenomenon of us climbers is a team going through a gear list obsessively and packing and repacking the bags and arguing whether to bring an extra #4 or double ropes or just a tag line, all the while tossing into our bags frustration, insecurity and misaligned expectation. Parting with our attachments is difficult, like trying to wean ourselves off an addiction. We do not get addicted for bad reasons. Addictions are often solutions to a problem. Addictions are part of our mental ecosystems because we created the soil for them to grow.

The closer you look, the sharper the knife. A Taoist parable of the butcher and the oxen explains:

"A good cook changes his knife once a year— because he cuts. A mediocre cook changes his knife once a month—because he hacks. I've had this knife of mine for nineteen years, and I've cut up thousands of oxen with it, and yet the blade is as good as though it had just come from the grindstone. There are spaces between the joints, and the blade of the knife has really no thickness. If you insert what has no thickness into such spaces, then there's plenty of room—more than enough for the blade to play about it. That's why after nineteen years the blade of my knife is still as good as when it first came from the grindstone."

You are the cook. The knife is your manner of navigating the world or climbing. The knife stays sharp the more you know how to work with the material you have inside and outside yourself.

Feedback Loops
Children are little liars, the better for it.

"The secrets of perfect swordsmanship consist in creating a certain frame or structure of mentality which is made always ready to respond instantly, that is, immediately, to what comes from the outside."

—*D.T. Suzuki, Japanese Buddhist monk and philosopher*

Children, the little liars they are, love the game of "telephone"—you know, that game where someone starts by saying something to someone and the message is carried around the circle until the final message is nothing like the original. Children get a kick out of it because it formalizes something they know intuitively, but which adults tend to forget ... namely, that miscommunication and deception are the norm. And that it's fun to bullshit someone.

An excessive amount of miscommunication is the bedrock of our world, a lot intentional, some not. Consider the postal service as it relates to timing. When shipped, the content of the letter remains unchanged, but it might arrive at different times, and a late arrival has real-world consequences. Communication isn't perfect because of the channels in which it works. We all know this with friends and lovers—the nature of the channel changes the message. We misread. We misinterpret. When you don't trust someone, it's hard for them to convince you they speak the truth. When it comes to our bodily communication systems, not only are the channels imperfect, what started as an inkling of doubt turned into trepidation when the thought was given time and space to grow. Then, that trepidation bonded with a lack of self-worth ... and you get the point. Things spiral. The process can take milliseconds or days, depending on the message and channel. Duration *is* content. A late letter rewrites itself.

As the phenomenon of choking, or botching it, exemplifies, athletes need to master these communicative lines of feedback on various levels: between their limbs, between their bodies and their thoughts, between rock and skin, between thoughts themselves. Between public exposure and vulnerability. Between athlete and coach.

As Suzuki, and Bruce Lee, observed about the martial arts (and it could be said of the climber): we need to create a "structure of mentality which is made always ready to respond instantly, that is, immediately, to what comes from the outside." Mastering feedback will make athletes better at what they do, encompassing sports performance psychologies such as situational awareness, field vision, and kinaesthetic mindfulness. Because all of these happen temporally, the shorter the duration, the quicker one's reactions, the speed of feedback often separates a gold medal from a bronze. It's not supposed to be easy.

Point A to Z

Between a ping and a notification is your personal history.

Every day, every second, the body/environment system is playing a game of telephone. Something is being communicated from point A to its destination at point Z. The problem is retaining the message's integrity, or, more exactly, the reasons for it to change tack, as it travels the vast network of our internal ecosystem.

I do a lot of mountain running, especially enjoying the downhills, and I really like to go fast until, of course, I am running down something steep and sketchy, and those little voices start to ping my awareness.

(Point A): *Slow down*, it says.
That talus is unstable.
A broken ankle here wouldhave you limping out for six hours.

Then another voice: *Jeez, dude, really? Slow down!*

Then the voice of indulgence: *But man, you are having so much fun. YOLO. Just a little longer.*

You've been cooped up all week at the office. Just run, for fuck's sake.

Then another: *Don't be an idiot. Break your ankle now, and you're out for the summer.*

Then another: *You're a skilled runner. You've never slowed down. No one could catch you at this rate.*

Your confidence builds.

Then you make a misstep.

You sprain an ankle (Point Z).

Point A had a truth based on the terrain, ability, and speed, but it changed as it traveled across voices, each with its own history. In any sport, especially for climbers, the chain needs to be understood by being broken, hacked or redirected. If you identify too strongly with the voice that always says "Go for it!", then you can't break free and see the other voices. In fact, identifying too strongly with any one voice is a violation of our basic nature.

Point A typically doesn't lie, as it tends to be reactionary, though points B to Y can convince you that point A is a scoundrel and that ignoring it is the best option. "A" is the event, and "Z" is the "best" reaction, but between the two is life filtering itself through concepts, ego attachments, ideas, pressures, in short, *everything*. Therein lies the problem and the Socratic task of knowing thyself.

To get clarity in climbing, it helps to have it in life. An honest megabyte of doubt at stage "G" can, when having gone through awareness at stage "M" that you always underestimate yourself, suddenly turns into overconfidence by the time you get to "Z." Which means you can convince yourself, against solid evidence to the contrary, that you should continue. Duration is content because duration adds complexity, and complexity forces a decision tree. In Buddhism, the idea of dependent origination says that all things arise in an interdependent fashion. Nothing arises on its own. No *thing* is an island unto itself. The principle works for minds—our mental ecologies are a result of our family life, landscape, friends—and this works on a smaller scale in terms of our mind-streams. In other words, the next event, A, is shaped by Z. Embodiment means not just being in your body, but embodying past failures, without blinders, with full honesty and transparency. It is a continuous Heraclitan stream, one in which compartmentalization is impossible. That you *cannot* compartmentalize illustrates another main principle of Buddhist thought: change is the only constant. Compartmentalization is an illusory understanding of the nature of being. The trite formula that "all you have is the present" might be great for taking a while, but disastrous in reality. We bring the past and present to each moment, and if we don't know what we are bringing, we will never be free. Free to live. Free to feel. Free to climb.

Pole Vaulters

The art of art is sensitivity.

Watch the video of Russian pole vaulter Yelena Isinbayeva on her record vault, and you will notice something. Her run seems normal. She plants the pole with focus. Her flight up is graceful, beautiful. She's fast, a faster runner than most. Remarkably, just milliseconds after she clears the bar, she is *already* celebrating, her arms bent, and fists *already* clenched in celebration. Even after having just completed a very complex series of movements, which required profound amounts of timing, max strength exertion, acute proprioception, and so on, her body has *already* communicated to her mind, registered the successful execution, and the message has been communicated to her emotional system to relax. She is smiling on the way down as if she just won the lottery. It's astonishing.

I watched the men's record of American-Swedish pole vaulter Armand Duplantis, and the same thing happened there. Immediate and unfiltered feedback loops are the fruit of awareness and developed embodiment. It is a practice, a craft, like Ondra cruxing out on an onsight and noticing the finer rubbings of chalk on the holds, so he knows which hand needs to latch what. The art of the hypersensitive, immediate feedback system is the mark of a Zen master, an artist and an athlete. It is the art *of art*, the mark of a mind freed. "To make people free is the aim of art," German artist Joseph Beuys said, "therefore art for me is the science of freedom."

Voices

Inside voices are personified drives and emotions. They are not your friends.

For athletes, consciousness is activated at every moment—the trick is to only activate the right ones (the ones appropriate to the task) at the right times (just when you need them). Blockages are points when the message deteriorates, and the mind fixates and the body stiffens.

The point, however, isn't so much to act as camp counselor to all the conflicting voices—since that is how the majority of stages will appear: as inside voices, personified drives and emotions with directives. It's noisy. Noise leads to confusion and bad decisions. Noise is not actionable information. The point isn't so much to get them to agree on a communications plan, though that is the first stage of many to mastering mind. In the end, the point is, like meditation, to not be attached to all the voices, to let them come and go, which is done by removing your ego and all its expectations from the driver's seat. At first, it's confusing. Some voices carry truth, while others only sprout from fear, or perhaps trauma is the origin of the insecurity. If we are not careful, the dominant voice becomes our personality because we identify with it. A lot of climbers project three grades above anything they will ever do because the feeling of working something harder somehow convinces them they are a better climber. Even though they are failing all the time, simply being on something hard supports a delusional sense of self. In this instance, that climber needs to deal with the voice of insecurity directly, and quieten it down, before they have a chance at quietening the overall mind-stream and changing their habit patterns, which will later change their neural patterns.

Venus Williams, one of the most decorated tennis players ever to have lived, is clear about where she got her mental strength. In an article for *The New York Times*, Williams writes, "But my body is only half of it. I still remember the first time my mother told me this: If I wanted to thrive in this sport—and in life—I needed to take care of my 'whole self.'" Part of her work was being kinder to herself, which is another way of saying she modified her self-talk and tampered down the cycles of negative feedback loops.

Some sports psychologists claim you need to talk to yourself with more kindness and not lash yourself with negative internal talk. Don't say, "You idiot!!" to yourself if you botch it; that is moralizing movement. Gallwey was insistent on this point. You'd never speak to a stranger or a friend that way, with such meanness. Kindness to self is a starting point, and most need to begin there. But, in time, the goal is to be rid of the voice altogether because voice is time, voice is distraction, voice is not *doing moves*. Doubt always sneaks through open doors.

The All

The alligator's skin is the water.

When you do anything in life, when you feel, when you climb, when you talk, you bring everything with you. It's a lot of stuff, most of it unnecessary, but it's there. It's inescapable. This goes for the old dualism of mind and body alike. Henri Bergson, Albert Whitehead and Gilles Deleuze, all philosophers interested in process, wrote at length of vitality defining all life, a compound effect where all beings and materialities are folded into future creations. The alligator's skin is the water: the cheetah, the savannah. "All that we are is the result of what we have thought," Siddhartha said. Or, "big mind experiences everything within itself."

Awareness is a labyrinth and can be daunting when first working navigating it. There's so much going on in our brains. What to listen to? What to act on? The first step is seeing and not acting.

After a while, you realize it is not a labyrinth. All our experience isn't forgotten or repressed, despite the myths of no-mind. Rather, *experience* needs to find a quiet home and do its work there, beneath the surface so that a well-trained somatic system stands on its shoulders and can perform, not necessarily the way we want it to, but the way it needs to. Because nothing is forgotten, everything is used. There is a philosophy of nature in the philosophy of climbing: each in its place, thriving, bringing forth vitality, what some ancient Greeks called justice. Climbing isn't a Zen activity, but it can be. Nothing is, in essence, a Zen activity. What makes a Zen activity is the practice you bring to it.

Debugging Instinct

Effortless, despite the cumbersome machinery.

"When I am on the wall, it is important not to be present rationally, but rather intuitively ... all decisions are made automatically."

Adam Ondra, Czech professional climber

Every time you talk to Alexa or Siri, hundreds of thousands of lines of code work feverishly behind the scenes to execute hundreds of different tasks, all within milliseconds, mostly without error.

First of all, the software distinguishes a talking human voice from a background voice through voice recognition. It then cancels the background noise and focuses on the voice alone. It judges whether a man or a woman is talking—a variable that influences search—and it transcribes the words you are saying. But not just words, it aims for meaning. When you ask about a "Van Morrison Sundance song," it knows very well you mean "Moondance," because thousands of others have made the same mistake and then found their way to "Moondance." The machine records this redirect and makes the assumption people mean one thing when they say another. It gives you what you *intended*. The list of coding tasks to arrive at a good search result are astonishing, which is why Google's search algorithms—the name for the formulas that operate the code—are highly guarded trade secrets, like the recipe for Pepsi.

After the software was developed, it went through hundreds of tests to improve its performance. Teams of engineers debugged the code and fixed mistakes. Bad software, say a beta version Google Maps, gets you lost, miscalibrates time, selects an inefficient path. It wastes your time. Yet, versions later, the final product is so good that it all appears effortless, a technological sublime, if you will, an erasure of the conditions of production. Pretty packaging hides the sweatshop, hides the algorithms, just as flow hides effort. Intelligence masked. It seems the computer is simply running on instinct, that it isn't thinking anymore, just automatic, but nothing could be further from the truth. Automation is very expensive, messy, and often breaks down. In 2018 Chinese public facial recognition software used to catch jaywalkers accidentally scanned the face of a wealthy businesswoman. The scanners had pulled the image from her face from the side of a bus. She was shamed in public before the mistake was caught ... but the point remains, the complexity behind all our modern world is bewildering, and we rarely notice it until it breaks down. Inside of all of us, we have our own form of software running invisibly, except that we are the coders *and* the software. So it is for *shokunin* climbers: effortless, despite the cumbersome machinery below the surface.

One of America's first climbing Olympians, Nathaniel Coleman, talks about how this invisible software works to get him to relax and focus: "I get this mixture of nerves and excitement. Elevated heart rate. All the classic signs of fight or flight response. But when a competition is going well, I think I'm just relaxing into a bath of positive emotions. And that's not something I have to focus on trying to do. It's something that just happens. And when I am in that state, my mind isn't thinking about the next boulder, or anything to come, or anything behind me ... I'm just happy to be in the moment."

Coleman says that it just happens, but, as with all top athletes, that happening has a history—it is the result of designed experience. Coleman has what Neumann terms "unconscious competence." He is aware that his poise *now* is a result of *then*. His past is integrated into his present in an automated manner, and so, going forward, he is less error prone. As Saint Exupéry says of the airplane, but which we can say of any elite athlete and the thousands of hours of training, "At the climax of its evolution, the machine conceals itself entirely." The machine is the designed mind-body interface.

Intuition

You do not exist for the sake of something else.

Zen is a fan of instinct, intuition, of circumventing the cumbersome machinery of human rationality so something else can be in the driver's seat. But this trust can be problematic.

Like our bodies, our intuition needs to be trained. It is not the case that there is a pure, honest, fully functioning intuition machine under our conscious mind-stream, which, if we only gave it the microphone, would talk us into spontaneous and free existence. That's a myth. There is no core inner voice, no pure ego that is creative and life-affirming. It takes work. Your sense of self is but a fleeting placeholder in your memory bank of sensations, personal history, body type, interactions, DNA, and so on. At the most basic level, you are becoming aware of what is growing in your consciousness, a life skill and climbing skill. At the next stage, you have to ask yourself why.

To be a whole climber, you need to be wholly involved, as Williams reminds us. When Michael Phelps asked: "Who was I, outside of the swimming pool?" he asked it with great wonder and honest intrigue. He put everything he had into his athletics, into time splits, gold medals and records. He was obsessed for years, but he is also the first to say it wasn't sustainable. One of the most decorated athletes of all time, Phelps became depressed. He had thoughts of killing himself, indicative of a lack of integration of his sporting life into the rest of his life. Gold medal ceremonies are momentary and fleeting, but you have to live with yourself forever. There are many different paths to the podium, and you can be a horrible, distracted SOB and motivated by pure ego and still dominate. But it catches up with you, and life is long. And the two are not mutually exclusive.

Why not become a better athlete via attentive practice and avoid all the pitfalls of self-worth in performance? Your existence *is* the point of your existence. There's no other point. Zen master Shunryu Suzuki writes: "We do not exist for the sake of something else."

The Myth of Mental Toughness

Mental toughness isn't about toughness or mentality.

Organic exertion. Mental minimalism. Breath. Breathing. Indifferent to success. Detached from failure. Awareness, presence, mindfulness. Relaxed intensity. Just moves. Calibration. Toggling without trauma. Deep patience. No interference. Letting the body and mind adapt. Right effort. Right movement. Right breath. Right attitude. Right tools ... and so on. Just concepts.

Rightness is not a feeling, nor an emotion, nor the end of a thought process. It is what you get when you climb mentally naked. Remove all the stuff that is *not* climbing, or allow in all that helps you climb, and no more. If you align all aspects—in life and training—to the goal of craft, of doing moves, then when it comes time, the things you bring to any athletic moment will be clean fuel, which means there will be no noise.

This is the work. This is perfection redefined. It's extremely difficult to master, a lifelong journey, but if you follow the body's cues and do the work, it will happen naturally over time. Deep satisfaction and contentment will replace frustration. You will climb better and with more consistency. The body's natural intelligence will, after constant practice, become the seat of intelligence. You will discover that what most sports psychologists call mental toughness isn't about toughness or mentality, as if mentality were just another type of uniform you put on before the game. Mentality is developed off the field, but expressed and refined on it. The optimum athletic mentality is developing a *pure relationality of body and mind* to the most efficient use of resources required for the rules of the game. When you do that, you will start to climb for the first time in your life. Your eyes will open in life as well: a convalescence.

· You will discover the power of subtraction. You will find, like Saint Exupéry, perfection is taking away. Or like Yuval Noah Hariri, author of the global bestseller *Sapiens*, who said the most important button on the keyboard is …"delete." That's right.

Final Act: The Zen Takeaway

Zen is the art of pruning to the essentials, to make room for new growth. Zen can be complex, contradictory, and sometimes infuriating to practice, but it is also a vast menu of wisdom. We all need to find our own recipe to approach and improve our attitude to, and in, climbing. Improvement is non-linear and idiosyncratic. The following short thoughts, practical in nature, are part of the Zen takeaway menu. Order what you will...

MIND: There is a stigma about mental training. Most climbers train their fingers and arms at least once a week, but how many times last month did you intentionally train your mind? Most likely, you don't know where to begin. To train the mind, take an approach just like you would anything else: target areas of concern, and work on them. Figure out what the problem is, whether it is fear, pressure or managing frustration, and apply the principles you learned here. Practice those principles on a weekly basis, both while climbing and in non-climbing scenarios. Go climbing, or warm up, not with the goal of warming up, or sending, but keeping a calm mind. Pay close attention to what is happening. Do this forever, because you are never done with this work.

CARE: Remember, no one cares about your climbing. No one cares about your social posts. Remove the notion that your climbing, and the routes you do, has any real significance. When you finally come to terms with this, you will *really* care about climbing and, for the first time, see it for what it *is*, not what climbing is *for you*.

MOMENT: Stop deluding yourself with false notions of completion. When you clip the chains or top a boulder, forget immediately that you did. Rather, pay close attention to the moment when you are ready to climb, or on the drive there. Better yet, the night before. This practice will cut short the long tail of priding yourself on accomplishment and develop the long game of preparation. Stop climbing to be accomplished and accomplishments will flow more naturally.

BREATHE: Do you drop from boulders, or hang on the rope after a fall, and notice you are out of breath? Being out of breath in climbing means you are not breathing properly. Start being mindful of your breathing. Basic meditation practice is this: Sit and breathe. Try only to breathe. Feel how much your mind is distracted by the way you are sitting, the sounds, the smells. Don't try to stop the thoughts. Next, do the same for climbing. Practice climbing only to be aware of your breath. At first, practice on warm-ups. Keep your attention on your in and out breaths. After you have mastered the art of breath on warm-ups, take it up a notch. You will see that it becomes harder to focus on breathing when the climbing gets more difficult, but that is not because it's ineffective; quite the opposite. To climb hard, you need to remove mental distraction and mental processes. Learning to stay focused on your breath is one of the quickest methods to accomplish this.

DISTRACTION: When climbing—before, during and after—minimize all forms of distraction. Put away your phone. Stop being annoyed by that barking dog. Stop chatting a few minutes before you climb. Get yourself out of the way. Before you get in the car, remind yourself to stay centered. When you arrive, the same thing. Focus on the natural beauty of the crag. Unless you are highly skilled, calming yourself down enough for a good performance 10 minutes before you tie in is impossible. You need a holistic approach, not a patchwork of hacks.

BALANCE: The next time you climb, feel the awkwardness, the off-balance moments. As Udo Neumann has noted, become conscious of your incompetence. Work with that awkwardness and inhabit it deeply. Pay attention to your body fighting it, then pay attention to your body accepting it. Be ok with being out of control. Do this often, and your range of comfort grows. Accepting it is a form of removing hesitation and blockages. For practice, try walking by putting the heel of one foot to your other toe, and so on like a chain, walking slowly. Breathe. Do this at work, or in your living room. It's a simple exercise, but, in addition to attention training, it shows you just how much the body is balancing itself on rote tasks. The awareness of the subtleties of balance will carry forward into climbing, a sport of balance. Zen masters have been doing this type of walking meditation for centuries.

EXPERIMENT: Do you know what it takes for you to be a good boulderer? A route climber? A crack or ice climber? Have you thought about the adjustments you need to make between the disciplines? If you don't, experiment. Always, always entertain new sequences and keep an open mind. Continue to tweak. Take risks. The slightest variations make all the difference when you are climbing at your limit. Stubbornness is attachment made visible.

DISBELIEF: Experiment with not believing. Try convincing yourself that you can't do something. Then try it. On a hard redpoint, try as little as possible until that moment when you realize you need to try. You will be surprised how little you need to try. Experiment with effort. Rev your body's engine. Learn to move in and out of exertion, and, most importantly, learn to ease out of effort. The closer you can return to a state of relaxed aggression the better. This is the art of calibration, JIT and the toggle.

MOTIVATE: Write down five things that motivate you about climbing, things that keep you coming back. Do any of your answers involve the simple act of climbing?

LOOK: All professional athletes watch footage of other athletes. Study top climbers and how they move, and don't. Figure out what habits you like about other's climbing, then try to bring that into your own. Notice how fast, or slowly, they move. Notice the calmness of top climbers, how easy it seems.

RELAX: Rather than doing hard moves all the time, work on mastering moves just a bit below your limit. This practice will eventually lead to making hard moves with more ease, because you have mastered the art of relaxing amidst difficulty.

FEAR: Calming nerves at the deepest levels takes time. To begin, simply start to notice them. Listen to what they are asking. Give them language and render their pings as information rather than noise that needs to be ignored. Notice their intensity. If out of fear you fall or tell your belayer to take in a moment of panic, sit with that fear and don't suppress it. Let your mind explore all the options that the fear presents. This is what the fear is trying to do: communicate with you. Go where the fear wants to go. Fear is a great teacher. Take it to the next level and analyze your climbing day before you go to bed. Be critical of your mental states. What worked? Why? What didn't work? Why? If you have fear, panic, or anxiety from a past trauma, introduce those same stressors carefully and diligently over a long period of time.

OTHERS: Notice those moments of watching another's shortcomings. You will surprise yourself how often your sense of feeling good about your climbing is only in relation to another. In contrast, notice how unencumbered the body feels when it is not climbing for something or someone else, or for a concept or idea you have attached to its performance.

FAILURE: After a crushing failure, ask your body what lesson it has for you. Think on that lesson. Carry that lesson forward to the next session or climb. Forgive your body if it makes a mistake. It will. Do not demean it. If necessary, only say things to yourself that you'd say to a good friend, or child. Eventually, the habit of negative self-talk will disappear altogether.

PROJECTS: Project to be inspired, either by the climb or the movement. Project because you want to master something. Project because you are an obsessive. Project because it brings you joy. Anything less is blasphemy. Purify your motives and walk away from your project if you are only climbing it for the grade.

GOALS: Stop pimping out your body's labor for cheap goals. Just stop. It cheapens the experience. Climb more without a goal in mind. This enables you to dwell longer in the realm of movement for movement's sake. Swap out high-intensity cycles for lower ones. The more you dwell in movement, the more you understand it. Climb volume to develop a deep catalogue of movement. Let those movements sink in as deep as you can.

SPEED: Slow down to speed up. Going too fast is often inefficient. Observe carefully what the holds are telling you about body position. It's a language. Don't expect to learn it quickly. It takes years, but you can always start now. Every climber has a style in the way they move. To get out of the rut, tinkering with speed is a good practice. Speed up or slow down. It will force your mind, and your body, into new patterns.

RISK: Have you asked yourself how much you are willing to risk? Pair the type of climbing you do with how much you are willing to risk. You will enjoy climbing more. Too much risk too early will only set you back, and your body will resist.

FATIGUE: When climbing, learn to detect not just the pump, but overall body fatigue. Overall body fatigue is a shadowy presence in climbing, the cause of a lot of our bad decisions. It is harder to pinpoint, but it is the reason our focus dulls. If you find your overall fitness is lacking, improve it immediately. Your climbing, endurance and decision-making will benefit within weeks.

MISTAKES: Embrace mistakes. In fact, try to create them. Use the wrong beta, or the wrong hold the wrong way, so as to generate a fight or flight response. Put yourself out of your routine. Stop conceiving weaknesses as threats.

FOCUS: Break down a hard climb of yours into micro-movements. Focus only on the first micro-movement, since when you climb at your limit, your ability to do an entire sequence is a result of how well you execute the first move, then the next. And so on. It's a game of accumulation. For practice, climb with as much bodily awareness as possible. Notice every foot placement, every swing of your torso. Try to overthink everything. In time, you will notice the limitations of supra-conscious bodily awareness.

REMOVE: Remove unnecessary effort so you can put right effort elsewhere. Don't just work smart, work as little as possible. Expend as little energy as possible. In running, it's called running economy. Top-tier route climbers instinctively find the easiest way to do something.

PRESSURE: Learning to perform under pressure is a skill. Start with matching pressure situations with low-hanging fruit, such that the consequences of not performing are not detrimental. Work on pure execution a good bit below your level. Once you have mastered the latter, only then move up in difficulty.

VISUALIZE: Visualise not just moves but states of bodily affairs. When you imagine yourself on something, try to tap into the feeling you will likely experience when up there. Do this enough and you will find that the feeling will lose intensity when you actually arrive, and thus, you will climb with greater poise.

Bibliography

Beilock SL, Carr TH. "On the fragility of skilled performance: what governs choking under pressure?" *Journal of Experimental Psychology.* 2001 Dec. 130(4).701-25.

Bergeron, Ben. *Chasing Excellence* (Lioncrest Publications, 2017).

Brown, Peter. *The Body and Society: Men, Women, and Sexual Renunciation in Early Christianity* (Columbia University Press, 2008).

Cashmore, Ellis. *Sport and Exercise Psychology: The Key Concepts* (Routledge, 2002).

Cuevas, Bryan J. and Jacqueline I. Stone. *The Buddhist Dead: Practices, Discourse, Representations* (University of Hawai'i Press, 2007).

Deleuze, Gilles. (1980) *Mille plateaux* (Minneapolis: University of Minnesota Press, 1987).
—*Spinoza: Philosophie pratique* (San Francisco: City Lights Books, 1988).
—*Francis Bacon: Logique de la sensation* (Minneapolis: University of Minnesota Press, 2005).

Derrida, Jacques. *On the Name* (Stanford University Press, 1995).

Etzel, Ken and Chelsea Jolly. *Rotpunct* (Patagonia Films, 2019).

Gallwey, Timothy. *The Inner Game of Tennis: The Classic Guide to the Mental Side of Peak Performance* (Random House Trade Paperbacks, 1997).

Gelb, David. *Jiro Dreams of Sushi* (Sundial Pictures, 2011).

Gill, John. "The Art of Bouldering," in the *American Alpine Journal* (1969).

Gould, Daniel, Kristen Dieffenbach and Aaron Moffett. "Psychological Characteristics and Their Development in Olympic Champions," in *Journal of Applied Sport Psychology*, 14:3, 172-204, 2002.

Griffiths RR, Richards WA, McCann U., Jesse R. "Psilocybin can occasion mystical-type experiences having substantial and sustained personal meaning and spiritual significance." *Psychopharmacology* (Berl). 2006 Aug;187(3):268-83.

Hanh, Thich Nhat. *The Heart of the Buddha's Teaching: Transforming Suffering Into Peace, Joy, and Liberation* (Harmony; 1st Broadway Books, 2015).

Hansen, Peter H. "Albert Smith, the Alpine Club, and the Invention of Mountaineering in Mid-Victorian Britain." *Journal of British Studies*, vol. 34, no. 3, [Cambridge University Press, North American Conference on British Studies], 1995, pp. 300–24.

Heidegger, Martin. *Being and Time*, trans. by John Macquarrie and Edward Robinson (London: SCM Press, 1962).

Hubel, D H. and T N Wiesel. "Receptive fields of single neurons in the cat's striate cortex." *The Journal of Physiology* .vol. 148,3 (1959): 574-91.

Huxley, Aldous. *The Doors of Perception* (Harper and Row, 1954).

Kamata, Shigeo, Kenji Shiimizu. *Zen and Aikido* (Aiki News, 1984).

LeBron, James and Maverick Carter. *The Playbook* (Netflix, 2020).

Lee, Bruce. *The Tao of Jeet Kune Do* (Black Belt Communications, 2011).

Longman, D., Stock, JT & Wells, JCK. "A trade-off between cognitive and physical performance, with relative preservation of brain function." *Sci Rep* 7, 13709 (2017).

Martinkova, Irena & Parry, Jim. "Zen and Sports: focusing on the quality of experiencing." In *Theology, Ethics and Transcendence in Sport*, pgs 211-222. (Routledge, 2010).

Macleod, Dave. *9 out of 10 Make the Same Mistakes* (Rare Breed Productions, 2009)

Muehlberger, Ellen. *Moment of Reckoning: Imagined Death and its Consequences in Late Ancient Christianity* (Oxford University Press, 2019).

Phelps, Michael, Brett Rapkin, Peter Carlisle and Michael O'Hara. *Weight of Gold* (HBO, 2020).

Rongjun, Yu. "Choking under pressure: the neuropsychological mechanisms of incentive-induced performance decrements," *Frontiers in Behavioral Neuroscience.* Vol 9, 2015.

Saint-Exupéry, Antoine de. *Wind, Sand and Stars* (New York: Reynal & Hitchcock, 1939).

Sanzaro, Francis. *Society Elsewhere: Why the Gravest Threat to Humanity Will Come From Within* (Zero Books, 2018)

—*The Boulder: A Philosophy for Bouldering* (Stone Country Press, 2011).

Simon, HA. "Designing organizations for an information-rich World." In *Computers, Communications, and the Public Interest*, pp. 38–52. (Baltimore: Johns Hopkins Press, 1971).

Suzuki, DT. *Buddha of Infinite Light: The Teachings of Shin Buddhism: the Japanese Way of Wisdom and Compassion* (Boulder: Shambhala; New Ed edition, 2002).

—*Zen and Japanese Culture* (New York: Bollingen/ Princeton University Press, 1970).

—*An Introduction to Zen Buddhism* (New York: Grove Press, p.9. 1964).

Acknowledgements

Like climbing, Zen belongs to no one. Still, I'd like to thank all the readers and writers in the Zen tradition for their loyalty to the craft of thinking, and, of course, not thinking. Bringing Zen to the West, in a responsible fashion, has been a decades-long enterprise, and ongoing. I hope to have contributed a small amount here.

I am indebted to my readers for their valuable feedback, in particular Tyler Stableford, Adrienne Cohen and Udo Neumann. Their insight led to much revision in the material. Thanks to John Gill as well for some crucial insight on key sections. Much thanks to my wife, Christy, and my kids, Amelia and Frankie, for their lovely chaos. Lastly, I'd like to thank John Watson and Sara Hunt for their support, commitment and fine eye for philosophical and publishing detail.

About the Author

Francis Sanzaro is equal parts climber, writer, and philosopher. The former Editor-in-Chief of *Rock and Ice*, *Ascent* and *Gym Climber* magazines, he has been climbing for more than thirty years: trad, ice, sport, alpine, and bouldering. His first book, *The Boulder: A Philosophy for Bouldering,* now in its second edition, won early critical acclaim. He has a PhD in the Philosophy of Religion (2012) from Syracuse University, New York. His essays, poetry and fiction have appeared frequently in *The New York Times, Outside, Climbing,* and *Adventure Journal,* among a dozen others. He has appeared on the BBC, on international podcasts, and has delivered a TEDx talk on wilderness and risk. He makes his home in the mountains of Colorado, with his wife and two children.

Find more IN THE MOMENT titles at saraband.net